POEMS,

BY

HENRY WADSWORTH LONGFELLOW.

IN TWO VOLUMES.

VOL. I.

A NEW EDITION.

BOSTON:

TICKNOR, REED, AND FIELDS.

M DCCC LIII.

CAMBRIDGE:
STEREOTYPED AND PRINTED BY
METCALF AND COMPANY,
PRINTERS TO THE UNIVERSITY.

CONTENTS OF VOL. I.

VOICES OF THE NIGHT.

BALLADS AND OTHER POEMS.

BALLADS.

MISCELLANEOUS.

POEMS ON SLAVERY.

THE SPANISH STUDENT.

VOICES OF THE NIGHT.

1840

PRELUDE.

PLEASANT it was, when woods were green,
   And winds were soft and low,
To lie amid some sylvan scene,
Where, the long drooping boughs between,
Shadows dark and sunlight sheen
   Alternate come and go ;

Or where the denser grove receives
   No sunlight from above,
But the dark foliage interweaves
In one unbroken roof of leaves,
Underneath whose sloping eaves
   The shadows hardly move.

Beneath some patriarchal tree
   I lay upon the ground ;
His hoary arms uplifted he,
And all the broad leaves over me
Clapped their little hands in glee,
   With one continuous sound ; —

A slumberous sound, — a sound that brings
   The feelings of a dream, —
As of innumerable wings,
As, when a bell no longer swings,
Faint the hollow murmur rings
   O'er meadow, lake, and stream.

And dreams of that which cannot die,
   Bright visions, came to me,
As lapped in thought I used to lie,
And gaze into the summer sky,
Where the sailing clouds went by,
   Like ships upon the sea ;

Dreams that the soul of youth engage
   Ere Fancy has been quelled ;
Old legends of the monkish page,
Traditions of the saint and sage,
Tales that have the rime of age,
   And chronicles of Eld.

And, loving still these quaint old themes,
   Even in the city's throng
I feel the freshness of the streams,
That, crossed by shades and sunny gleams,
Water the green land of dreams,
   The holy land of song.

Therefore, at Pentecost, which brings
   The Spring, clothed like a bride,
When nestling buds unfold their wings,
And bishop's-caps have golden rings,
Musing upon many things,
   I sought the woodlands wide.

The green trees whispered low and mild ;
   It was a sound of joy !
They were my playmates when a child,
And rocked me in their arms so wild !
Still they looked at me and smiled,
    As if I were a boy ;

And ever whispered, mild and low,
    " Come, be a child once more ! "
And waved their long arms to and fro,
And beckoned solemnly and slow ;
O, I could not choose but go
    Into the woodlands hoar ;

Into the blithe and breathing air,
    Into the solemn wood,
Solemn and silent everywhere !
Nature with folded hands seemed there,
Kneeling at her evening prayer !
    Like one in prayer I stood.

Before me rose an avenue
   Of tall and sombrous pines ;
Abroad their fan-like branches grew,
And, where the sunshine darted through,
Spread a vapor soft and blue,
   In long and sloping lines.

And, falling on my weary brain,
   Like a fast-falling shower,
The dreams of youth came back again ;
Low lispings of the summer rain,
Dropping on the ripened grain,
   As once upon the flower.

Visions of childhood ! Stay, O stay '
   Ye were so sweet and wild !
And distant voices seemed to say,
" It cannot be ! They pass away !
Other themes demand thy lay ;
   Thou art no more a child !

"The land of Song within thee lies,
    Watered by living springs ;
The lids of Fancy's sleepless eyes
Are gates unto that Paradise,
Holy thoughts, like stars, arise,
    Its clouds are angels' wings.

"Learn, that henceforth thy song shall be,
    Not mountains capped with snow,
Nor forests sounding like the sea,
Nor rivers flowing ceaselessly,
Where the woodlands bend to see
    The bending heavens below.

"There is a forest where the din
    Of iron branches sounds !
A mighty river roars between,
And whosoever looks therein,
Sees the heavens all black with sin, —
    Sees not its depths, nor bounds.

" Athwart the swinging branches cast,
    Soft rays of sunshine pour ;
  Then comes the fearful wintry blast ;
  Our hopes, like withered leaves, fall fast ;
  Pallid lips say, ' It is past !
    We can return no more ! '

" Look, then, into thine heart, and write !
    Yes, into Life's deep stream !
  All forms of sorrow and delight,
  All solemn Voices of the Night,
  That can soothe thee, or affright, —
    Be these henceforth thy theme "

VOICES OF THE NIGHT.

Πότνια, πότνια νύξ,
ὑπνοδότειρα τῶν πολυπόνων βροτῶν,
Ἐρεβόθεν ἴθι· μόλε μόλε κατάπτερος
Ἀγαμεμνόνιον ἐπὶ δόμον·
ὑπὸ γὰρ ἀλγέων, ὑπό τε συμφορᾶς
διοιχόμεθ᾽, οἰχόμεθα.

EURIPIDES.

HYMN TO THE NIGHT.

Ἀσπασίη, τρίλλιστος.

I HEARD the trailing garments of the Night
    Sweep through her marble halls !
I saw her sable skirts all fringed with light
    From the celestial walls !

I felt her presence, by its spell of might,
    Stoop o'er me from above ;
The calm, majestic presence of the Night,
    As of the one I love.

I heard the sounds of sorrow and delight,
    The manifold, soft chimes,
That fill the haunted chambers of the Night,
    Like some old poet's rhymes.

From the cool cisterns of the midnight air
    My spirit drank repose;
The fountain of perpetual peace flows there, —
    From those deep cisterns flows.

O holy Night! from thee I learn to bear
    What man has borne before!
Thou layest thy finger on the lips of Care,
    And they complain no more.

Peace! Peace! Orestes-like I breathe this prayer!
    Descend with broad-winged flight,
The welcome, the thrice-prayed for, the most fair,
    The best-beloved Night!

A PSALM OF LIFE.

WHAT THE HEART OF THE YOUNG MAN SAID TO THE PSALMIST.

TELL me not, in mournful numbers,
"Life is but an empty dream!"
For the soul is dead that slumbers,
And things are not what they seem.

Life is real! Life is earnest!
And the grave is not its goal ;
"Dust thou art, to dust returnest,"
Was not spoken of the soul.

Not enjoyment, and not sorrow,
    Is our destined end or way ;
But to act, that each to-morrow
    Find us farther than to-day.

Art is long, and Time is fleeting,
    And our hearts, though stout and brave,
Still, like muffled drums, are beating
    Funeral marches to the grave.

In the world's broad field of battle
    In the bivouac of Life,
Be not like dumb, driven cattle !
    Be a hero in the strife !

Trust no Future, howe'er pleasant !
    Let the dead Past bury its dead !
Act, — act in the living Present !
    Heart within, and God o'erhead !

Lives of great men all remind us
   We can make our lives sublime,
And, departing, leave behind us
   Footprints on the sands of time ;

Footprints, that perhaps another,
   Sailing o'er life's solemn main,
A forlorn and shipwrecked brother,
   Seeing, shall take heart again.

Let us, then, be up and doing,
   With a heart for any fate ;
Still achieving, still pursuing,
   Learn to labor and to wait.

THE REAPER AND THE FLOWERS.

THERE is a Reaper, whose name is Death,
  And, with his sickle keen,
He reaps the bearded grain at a breath,
  And the flowers that grow between.

" Shall I have nought that is fair ? " saith he ;
  " Have nought but the bearded grain ?
Though the breath of these flowers is sweet to me,
  I will give them all back again."

He gazed at the flowers with tearful eyes,
    He kissed their drooping leaves ;
It was for the Lord of Paradise
    He bound them in his sheaves.

" My Lord has need of these flowerets gay,"
    The Reaper said, and smiled ;
" Dear tokens of the earth are they,
    Where he was once a child.

" They shall all bloom in fields of light,
    Transplanted by my care,
And saints, upon their garments white,
    These sacred blossoms wear."

And the mother gave, in tears and pain,
    The flowers she most did love ;
She knew she should find them all again
    In the fields of light above.

O, not in cruelty, not in wrath,
    The Reaper came that day ;
'T was an angel visited the green earth,
    And took the flowers away.

THE LIGHT OF STARS.

THE night is come, but not too soon;
   And sinking silently,
All silently, the little moon
   Drops down behind the sky.

There is no light in earth or heaven,
   But the cold light of stars;
And the first watch of night is given
   To the red planet Mars.

Is it the tender star of love ?
　The star of love and dreams ?
O no ! from that blue tent above,
　A hero's armour gleams.

And earnest thoughts within me rise,
　When I behold afar,
Suspended in the evening skies,
　The shield of that red star.

O star of strength ! I see thee stand
　And smile upon my pain ;
Thou beckonest with thy mailed hand,
　And I am strong again.

Within my breast there is no light,
　But the cold light of stars ;
I give the first watch of the night
　To the red planet Mars.

The star of the unconquered will,
   He rises in my breast,
Serene, and resolute, and still,
   And calm, and self-possessed.

And thou, too, whosoe'er thou art,
   That readest this brief psalm,
As one by one thy hopes depart,
   Be resolute and calm.

O fear not in a world like this,
   And thou shalt know ere long,
Know how sublime a thing it is
   To suffer and be strong.

FOOTSTEPS OF ANGELS.

WHEN the hours of Day are numbered,
  And the voices of the Night
Wake the better soul, that slumbered,
  To a holy, calm delight ;

Ere the evening lamps are lighted,
  And, like phantoms grim and tall,
Shadows from the fitful fire-light
  Dance upon the parlour wall ;

Then the forms of the departed
   Enter at the open door ;
The beloved, the true-hearted,
   Come to visit me once more ;

He, the young and strong, who cherished
   Noble longings for the strife,
By the road-side fell and perished,
   Weary with the march of life !

They, the holy ones and weakly,
   Who the cross of suffering bore,
Folded their pale hands so meekly,
   Spake with us on earth no more !

And with them the Being Beauteous,
   Who unto my youth was given,
More than all things else to love me,
   And is now a saint in heaven.

With a slow and noiseless footstep
　Comes that messenger divine,
Takes the vacant chair beside me,
　Lays her gentle hand in mine.

And she sits and gazes at me
　With those deep and tender eyes,
Like the stars, so still and saint-like,
　Looking downward from the skies

Uttered not, yet comprehended,
　Is the spirit's voiceless prayer,
Soft rebukes, in blessings ended,
　Breathing from her lips of air.

O, though oft depressed and lonely,
　All my fears are laid aside,
If I but remember only
　Such as these have lived and died !

17

FLOWERS.

Spake full well, in language quaint and olden,
   One who dwelleth by the castled Rhine,
When he called the flowers, so blue and golden,
   Stars, that in earth's firmament do shine.

Stars they are, wherein we read our history,
   As astrologers and seers of eld ;
Yet not wrapped about with awful mystery,
   Like the burning stars, which they beheld.

2

Wondrous truths, and manifold as wondrous,
    God hath written in those stars above ;
But not less in the bright flowerets under us
    Stands the revelation of his love.

Bright and glorious is that revelation,
    Written all over this great world of ours ;
Making evident our own creation,
    In these stars of earth, — these golden flowers.

And the Poet, faithful and far-seeing,
    Sees, alike in stars and flowers, a part
Of the self-same, universal being,
    Which is throbbing in his brain and heart.

Gorgeous flowerets in the sunlight shining,
    Blossoms flaunting in the eye of day,
Tremulous leaves, with soft and silver lining,
    Buds that open only to decay ;

Brilliant hopes, all woven in gorgeous tissues,
    Flaunting gayly in the golden light ;
Large desires, with most uncertain issues,
    Tender wishes, blossoming at night !

These in flowers and men are more than seeming ,
    Workings are they of the self-same powers,
Which the Poet, in no idle dreaming,
    Seeth in himself and in the flowers.

Everywhere about us are they glowing,
    Some like stars, to tell us Spring is born ;
Others, their blue eyes with tears o'erflowing,
    Stand like Ruth amid the golden corn ;

Not alone in Spring's armorial bearing,
    And in Summer's green-emblazoned field,
But in arms of brave old Autumn's wearing,
    In the centre of his brazen shield ;

Not alone in meadows and green alleys,
   On the mountain-top, and by the brink
Of sequestered pools in woodland valleys,
   Where the slaves of Nature stoop to drink ;

Not alone in her vast dome of glory,
   Not on graves of bird and beast alone,
But in old cathedrals, high and hoary,
   On the tombs of heroes, carved in stone ;

In the cottage of the rudest peasant,
   In ancestral homes, whose crumbling towers,
Speaking of the Past unto the Present,
   Tell us of the ancient Games of Flowers ;

In all places, then, and in all seasons,
   Flowers expand their light and soul-like wings,
Teaching us, by most persuasive reasons,
   How akin they are to human things.

And with childlike, credulous affection
　We behold their tender buds expand ;
Emblems of our own great resurrection,
　Emblems of the bright and better land.

THE BELEAGUERED CITY.

I HAVE read, in some old marvellous tale,
  Some legend strange and vague,
That a midnight host of spectres pale
  Beleaguered the walls of Prague.

Beside the Moldau's rushing stream,
  With the wan moon overhead,
There stood, as in an awful dream,
  The army of the dead.

White as a sea-fog, landward bound,
　　The spectral camp was seen,
And, with a sorrowful, deep sound,
　　The river flowed between.

No other voice nor sound was there,
　　No drum, nor sentry's pace ;
The mist-like banners clasped the air,
　　As clouds with clouds embrace.

But, when the old cathedral bell
　　Proclaimed the morning prayer,
The white pavilions rose and fell
　　On the alarmed air.

Down the broad valley fast and far
　　The troubled army fled ;
Up rose the glorious morning star,
　　The ghastly host was dead.

I have read, in the marvellous heart of man,
    That strange and mystic scroll,
That an army of phantoms vast and wan
    Beleaguer the human soul.

Encamped beside Life's rushing stream,
    In Fancy's misty light,
Gigantic shapes and shadows gleam
    Portentous through the night.

Upon its midnight battle-ground
    The spectral camp is seen,
And, with a sorrowful, deep sound,
    Flows the River of Life between.

No other voice, nor sound is there,
    In the army of the grave ;
No other challenge breaks the air,
    But the rushing of Life's wave.

And, when the solemn and deep church-bell
    Entreats the soul to pray,
The midnight phantoms feel the spell,
    The shadows sweep away.

Down the broad Vale of Tears afar
    The spectral camp is fled;
Faith shineth as a morning star,
    Our ghastly fears are dead.

MIDNIGHT MASS FOR THE DYING YEAR.

Yes, the Year is growing old,
    And his eye is pale and bleared !
Death, with frosty hand and cold,
    Plucks the old man by the beard,
        Sorely, — sorely !

The leaves are falling, falling,
    Solemnly and slow ;
Caw ! caw ! the rooks are calling,
    It is a sound of woe,
        A sound of woe !

Through woods and mountain passes
   The winds, like anthems, roll ;
They are chanting solemn masses,
   Singing ; " Pray for this poor soul,
      Pray, — pray ! "

And the hooded clouds, like friars,
   Tell their beads in drops of rain,
And patter their doleful prayers ; —
   But their prayers are all in vain,
      All in vain !

There he stands in the foul weather,
   The foolish, fond Old Year,
Crowned with wild flowers and with heather,
   Like weak, despised Lear,
      A king, — a king !

Then comes the summer-like day,
   Bids the old man rejoice !
His joy ! his last ! O, the old man gray,
   Loveth that ever-soft voice,
      Gentle and low.

To the crimson woods he saith, —
   To the voice gentle and low
Of the soft air, like a daughter's breath,—
   " Pray do not mock me so !
      Do not laugh at me ! "

And now the sweet day is dead ;
   Cold in his arms it lies ;
No stain from its breath is spread
   Over the glassy skies,
      No mist or stain !

Then, too, the Old Year dieth,
   And the forests utter a moan,
Like the voice of one who crieth
   In the wilderness alone,
      " Vex not his ghost ! "

Then comes, with an awful roar,
   Gathering and sounding on,
The storm-wind from Labrador,
   The wind Euroclydon,
      The storm-wind !

Howl ! howl ! and from the forest
   Sweep the red leaves away !
Would, the sins that thou abhorrest,
   O Soul ! could thus decay,
      And be swept away !

For there shall come a mightier blast,
  There shall be a darker day ;
And the stars, from heaven down-cast,
  Like red leaves be swept away !
    Kyrie, eleyson !
    Christe, eleyson !

EARLIER POEMS.

[These poems were written for the most part during my college life, and all of them before the age of nineteen. Some have found their way into schools, and seem to be successful. Others lead a vagabond and precarious existence in the corners of newspapers; or have changed their names and run away to seek their fortunes beyond the sea. I say, with the Bishop of Avranches, on a similar occasion; " I cannot be displeased to see these children of mine, which I have neglected, and almost exposed, brought from their wanderings in lanes and alleys, and safely lodged, in order to go forth into the world together in a more decorous garb."]

AN APRIL DAY.

WHEN the warm sun, that brings
Seed-time and harvest, has returned again,
'T is sweet to visit the still wood, where springs
  The first flower of the plain.

I love the season well,
When forest glades are teeming with bright forms,
Nor dark and many-folded clouds foretell
  The coming-on of storms.

From the earth's loosened mould
The sapling draws its sustenance, and thrives ;
Though stricken to the heart with winter's cold,
　　The drooping tree revives.

　　The softly-warbled song
Comes from the pleasant woods, and colored wings
Glance quick in the bright sun, that moves along
　　The forest openings.

When the bright sunset fills
The silver woods with light, the green slope throws
Its shadows in the hollows of the hills,
　　And wide the upland glows.

　　And, when the eve is born,
In the blue lake the sky, o'er-reaching far,
Is hollowed out, and the moon dips her horn,
　　And twinkles many a star.

Inverted in the tide,
Stand the gray rocks, and trembling shadows throw,
And the fair trees look over, side by side,
    And see themselves below.

    Sweet April!—many a thought
Is wedded unto thee, as hearts are wed ;
Nor shall they fail, till, to its autumn brought,
    Life's golden fruit is shed.

AUTUMN.

———

With what a glory comes and goes the year !
The buds of spring, those beautiful harbingers
Of sunny skies and cloudless times, enjoy
Life's newness, and earth's garniture spread out
And when the silver habit of the clouds
Comes down upon the autumn sun, and with
A sober gladness the old year takes up
His bright inheritance of golden fruits,
A pomp and pageant fill the splendid scene.

There is a beautiful spirit breathing now
Its mellow richness on the clustered trees,
And, from a beaker full of richest dyes,
Pouring new glory on the autumn woods,
And dipping in warm light the pillared clouds.
Morn on the mountain, like a summer bird,
Lifts up her purple wing, and in the vales
The gentle wind, a sweet and passionate wooer,
Kisses the blushing leaf, and stirs up life
Within the solemn woods of ash deep-crimsoned,
And silver beech, and maple yellow-leaved,
Where autumn, like a faint old man, sits down
By the wayside a-weary.   Through the trees
The golden robin moves.   The purple finch,
That on wild cherry and red cedar feeds,
A winter bird, comes with its plaintive whistle,
And pecks by the witch-hazel, whilst aloud
From cottage roofs the warbling blue-bird sings,
And merrily, with oft-repeated stroke,
Sounds from the threshing-floor the busy flail.

O what a glory doth this world put on
For him who, with a fervent heart, goes forth
Under the bright and glorious sky, and looks
On duties well performed, and days well spent!
For him the wind, ay, and the yellow leaves
Shall have a voice, and give him eloquent teachings.
He shall so hear the solemn hymn, that Death
Has lifted up for all, that he shall go
To his long resting-place without a tear.

WOODS IN WINTER.

WHEN winter winds are piercing chill,
   And through the hawthorn blows the gale
With solemn feet I tread the hill,
   That overbrows the lonely vale.

O'er the bare upland, and away
   Through the long reach of desert woods,
The embracing sunbeams chastely play,
   And gladden these deep solitudes.

Where, twisted round the barren oak,
  The summer vine in beauty clung,
And summer winds the stillness broke,
  The crystal icicle is hung.

Where, from their frozen urns, mute springs
  Pour out the river's gradual tide,
Shrilly the skater's iron rings,
  And voices fill the woodland side.

Alas ! how changed from the fair scene,
  When birds sang out their mellow lay,
And winds were soft, and woods were green,
  And the song ceased not with the day.

But still wild music is abroad,
  Pale, desert woods ! within your crowd ;
And gathering winds, in hoarse accord,
  Amid the vocal reeds pipe loud.

Chill airs and wintry winds ! my ear
   Has grown familiar with your song ;
I hear it in the opening year, —
   I listen, and it cheers me long

HYMN

OF THE MORAVIAN NUNS OF BETHLEHEM,

AT THE CONSECRATION OF PULASKI'S BANNER.

WHEN the dying flame of day
Through the chancel shot its ray,
Far the glimmering tapers shed
Faint light on the cowled head ;
And the censer burning swung,
Where, before the altar, hung
The blood-red banner, that with prayer
Had been consecrated there.

And the nun's sweet hymn was heard the while,
Sung low in the dim, mysterious aisle.

    " Take thy banner !   May it wave
       Proudly o'er the good and brave ;
       When the battle's distant wail
       Breaks the sabbath of our vale,
       When the clarion's music thrills
       To the hearts of these lone hills,
       When the spear in conflict shakes,
       And the strong lance shivering breaks.

    " Take thy banner ! and, beneath
       The battle-cloud's encircling wreath,
       Guard it ! — till our homes are free !
       Guard it ! — God will prosper thee !
       In the dark and trying hour,
       In the breaking forth of power,
       In the rush of steeds and men,
       His right hand will shield thee then.

" Take thy banner !   But, when night
Closes round the ghastly fight,
If the vanquished warrior bow,
Spare him ! — By our holy vow,
By our prayers and many tears,
By the mercy that endears,
Spare him ! — he our love hath shared !
Spare him ! — as thou wouldst be spared !

" Take thy banner ! — and if e'er
Thou shouldst press the soldier's bier,
And the muffled drum should beat
To the tread of mournful feet,
Then this crimson flag shall be
Martial cloak and shroud for thee."

The warrior took that banner proud,
And it was his martial cloak and shroud !

SUNRISE ON THE HILLS.

I STOOD upon the hills, when heaven's wide arch
Was glorious with the sun's returning march,
And woods were brightened, and soft gales
Went forth to kiss the sun-clad vales.
The clouds were far beneath me; — bathed in light,
They gathered mid-way round the wooded height,
And, in their fading-glory, shone
Like hosts in battle overthrown,
As many a pinnacle, with shifting glance,
Through the gray mist thrust up its shattered lance,

And rocking on the cliff was left
The dark pine blasted, bare, and cleft.
The veil of cloud was lifted, and below
Glowed the rich valley, and the river's flow
Was darkened by the forest's shade,
Or glistened in the white cascade ;
Where upward, in the mellow blush of day,
The noisy bittern wheeled his spiral way.

I heard the distant waters dash,
I saw the current whirl and flash, —
And richly, by the blue lake's silver beach,
The woods were bending with a silent reach.
Then o'er the vale, with gentle swell,
The music of the village bell
Came sweetly to the echo-giving hills ;
And the wild horn, whose voice the woodland fills,
Was ringing to the merry shout,
That faint and far the glen sent out,

Where, answering to the sudden shot, thin smoke,
Through thick-leaved branches, from the dingle
    broke.

  If thou art worn and hard beset
With sorrows, that thou wouldst forget,
If thou wouldst read a lesson, that will keep
Thy heart from fainting and thy soul from sleep,
Go to the woods and hills ! — No tears
Dim the sweet look that Nature wears.

THE SPIRIT OF POETRY.

THERE is a quiet spirit in these woods,
That dwells where'er the gentle south wind blows;
Where, underneath the white-thorn, in the glade,
The wild flowers bloom, or, kissing the soft air,
The leaves above their sunny palms outspread.
With what a tender and impassioned voice
It fills the nice and delicate ear of thought,
When the fast-ushering star of morning comes
O'er-riding the gray hills with golden scarf;

Or when the cowled and dusky-sandaled Eve,
In mourning weeds, from out the western gate,
Departs with silent pace !   That spirit moves
In the green valley, where the silver brook,
From its full laver, pours the white cascade ;
And, babbling low amid the tangled woods,
Slips down through moss-grown stones with end-
        less laughter.
And frequent, on the everlasting hills,
Its feet go forth, when it doth wrap itself
In all the dark embroidery of the storm,
And shouts the stern, strong wind. And here, amid
The silent majesty of these deep woods,
Its presence shall uplift thy thoughts from earth,
As to the sunshine and the pure, bright air
Their tops the green trees lift. Hence gifted bards
Have ever loved the calm and quiet shades.
For them there was an eloquent voice in all
The sylvan pomp of woods, the golden sun,

4

The flowers, the leaves, the river on its way,
Blue skies, and silver clouds, and gentle winds, —
The swelling upland, where the sidelong sun
Aslant the wooded slope, at evening, goes, —
Groves, through whose broken roof the sky looks in,
Mountain, and shattered cliff, and sunny vale,
The distant lake, fountains, — and mighty trees,
In many a lazy syllable, repeating
Their old poetic legends to the wind.

And this is the sweet spirit, that doth fill
The world; and, in these wayward days of youth,
My busy fancy oft embodies it,
As a bright image of the light and beauty
That dwell in nature, — of the heavenly forms
We worship in our dreams, and the soft hues
That stain the wild bird's wing, and flush the clouds
When the sun sets.   Within her eye
The heaven of April, with its changing light,

And when it wears the blue of May, is hung,
And on her lip the rich, red rose.   Her hair
Is like the summer tresses of the trees,
When twilight makes them brown, and on her
        cheek
Blushes the richness of an autumn sky,
With ever-shifting beauty.   Then her breath,
It is so like the gentle air of Spring,
As, from the morning's dewy flowers, it comes
Full of their fragrance, that it is a joy
To have it round us, — and her silver voice
Is the rich music of a summer bird,
Heard in the still night, with its passionate ca-
        dence.

BURIAL OF THE MINNISINK.

On sunny slope and beechen swell,
The shadowed light of evening fell ;
And, where the maple's leaf was brown,
With soft and silent lapse came down
The glory, that the wood receives,
At sunset, in its brazen leaves.

Far upward in the mellow light
Rose the blue hills.   One cloud of white,

Around a far uplifted cone,
In the warm blush of evening shone ;
An image of the silver lakes,
By which the Indian's soul awakes.

But soon a funeral hymn was heard
Where the soft breath of evening stirred
The tall, gray forest ; and a band
Of stern in heart, and strong in hand,
Came winding down beside the wave,
To lay the red chief in his grave.

They sang, that by his native bowers
He stood, in the last moon of flowers,
And thirty snows had not yet shed
Their glory on the warrior's head ;
But, as the summer fruit decays,
So died he in those naked days.

A dark cloak of the roebuck's skin
Covered the warrior, and within
Its heavy folds the weapons, made
For the hard toils of war, were laid ;
The cuirass, woven of plaited reeds,
And the broad belt of shells and beads.

Before, a dark-haired virgin train
Chanted the death dirge of the slain ;
Behind, the long procession came
Of hoary men and chiefs of fame,
With heavy hearts, and eyes of grief,
Leading the war-horse of their chief.

Stripped of his proud and martial dress,
Uncurbed, unreined, and riderless,
With darting eye, and nostril spread,
And heavy and impatient tread,
He came ; and oft that eye so proud
Asked for his rider in the crowd.

They buried the dark chief they freed
Beside the grave his battle steed ;
And swift an arrow cleaved its way
To his stern heart ! One piercing neigh
Arose, — and, on the dead man's plain,
The rider grasps his steed again.

TRANSLATIONS.

[Don Jorge Manrique, the author of the following poem, flourished in the last half of the fifteenth century. He followed the profession of arms, and died on the field of battle. Mariana, in his History of Spain, makes honorable mention of him, as being present at the siege of Uclés; and speaks of him as "a youth of estimable qualities, who in this war gave brilliant proofs of his valor. He died young; and was thus cut off from long exercising his great virtues, and exhibiting to the world the light of his genius, which was already known to fame." He was mortally wounded in a skirmish near Cañavete, in in the year 1479.

The name of Rodrigo Manrique, the father of the poet, Conde de Paredes and Maestre de Santiago, is well known in Spanish history and song. He died in 1476; according to Mariana, in the town of Uclés; but, according to the poem of his son, in Ocaña. It was his death that called forth the poem upon which rests the literary reputation of the younger Manrique. In the language of his historian, "Don Jorge Manrique, in an elegant Ode, full of poetic beauties, rich embellishments of genius, and high moral reflections, mourned the death of his father as with a funeral hymn." This praise is not exaggerated. The poem is a model in its kind. Its conception is solemn and beautiful; and, in accordance with it, the style moves on — calm, dignified, and majestic.]

COPLAS DE MANRIQUE.

FROM THE SPANISH.

O LET the soul her slumbers break,
Let thought be quickened, and awake ;
Awake to see
How soon this life is past and gone,
And death comes softly stealing on,
How silently !

Swiftly our pleasures glide away,
Our hearts recall the distant day
With many sighs ;
The moments that are speeding fast
We heed not, but the past, — the past, —
More highly prize.

Onward its course the present keeps,
Onward the constant current sweeps,
Till life is done ;
And, did we judge of time aright,
The past and future in their flight
Would be as one.

Let no one fondly dream again,
That Hope and all her shadowy train
Will not decay ;
Fleeting as were the dreams of old,
Remembered like a tale that 's told,
They pass away.

Our lives are rivers, gliding free
To that unfathomed, boundless sea,
The silent grave !
Thither all earthly pomp and boast
Roll, to be swallowed up and lost
In one dark wave.

Thither the mighty torrents stray,
Thither the brook pursues its way,
And tinkling rill.
There all are equal.   Side by side
The poor man and the son of pride
Lie calm and still.

I will not here invoke the throng
Of orators and sons of song,
The deathless few ;
Fiction entices and deceives,
And, sprinkled o'er her fragrant leaves,
Lies poisonous dew.

To One alone my thoughts arise,
The Eternal Truth,—the Good and Wise,—
To Him I cry,
Who shared on earth our common lot,
But the world comprehended not
His deity.

This world is but the rugged road
Which leads us to the bright abode
Of peace above ;
So let us· choose that narrow way,
Which leads no traveller's foot astray
From realms of love.

Our cradle is the starting-place,
In life we run the onward race,
And reach the goal ;
When, in the mansions of the blest,
Death leaves to its eternal rest
The weary soul.

Did we but use it as we ought,
This world would school each wandering
To its high state.   [thought
Faith wings the soul beyond the sky,
Up to that better world on high,
For which we wait.

Yes, — the glad messenger of love,
To guide us to our home above,
The Saviour came ;
Born amid mortal cares and fears,
He suffered in this vale of tears
A death of shame.

Behold of what delusive worth
The bubbles we pursue on earth,
The shapes we chase,
Amid a world of treachery !
They vanish ere death shuts the eye,
And leave no trace.

Time steals them from us, — chances strange,
Disastrous accidents, and change,
That come to all ;
Even in the most exalted state,
Relentless sweeps the stroke of fate ;
The strongest fall.

Tell me, — the charms that lovers seek
In the clear eye and blushing cheek,
The hues that play
O'er rosy lip and brow of snow,
When hoary age approaches slow,
Ah, where are they ?

The cunning skill, the curious arts,
The glorious strength that youth imparts
In life's first stage ;
These shall become a heavy weight,
When Time swings wide his outward gate
To weary age.

The noble blood of Gothic name,
Heroes emblazoned high to fame,
In long array ;
How, in the onward course of time,
The landmarks of that race sublime
Were swept away !

Some, the degraded slaves of lust,
Prostrate and trampled in the dust,
Shall rise no more ;
Others, by guilt and crime, maintain
The scutcheon, that, without a stain,
Their fathers bore.

Wealth and the high estate of pride,
With what untimely speed they glide,
How soon depart !
Bid not the shadowy phantoms stay,
The vassals of a mistress they,
Of fickle heart.

These gifts in Fortune's hands are found ;
Her swift revolving wheel turns round,
And they are gone !
No rest the inconstant goddess knows,
But changing, and without repose,
Still hurries on.

5

Even could the hand of avarice save
Its gilded baubles, till the grave
Reclaimed its prey,
Let none on such poor hopes rely ;
Life, like an empty dream, flits by,
And where are they ?

Earthly desires and sensual lust
Are passions springing from the dust, —
They fade and die ;
But, in the life beyond the tomb,
They seal the immortal spirit's doom
Eternally !

The pleasures and delights, which mask
In treacherous smiles life's serious task,
What are they, all,
But the fleet coursers of the chase,
And death an ambush in the race,
Wherein we fall ?

No foe, no dangerous pass, we heed,
Brook no delay, — but onward speed
With loosened rein ;
And, when the fatal snare is near,
We strive to check our mad career,
But strive in vain.

Could we new charms to age impart,
And fashion with a cunning art
The human face,
As we can clothe the soul with light,
And make the glorious spirit bright
With heavenly grace, —

How busily each passing hour
Should we exert that magic power.
What ardor show,
To deck the sensual slave of sin,
Yet leave the freeborn soul within,
In weeds of woe !

Monarchs, the powerful and the strong,
Famous in history and in song
Of olden time,
Saw, by the stern decrees of fate,
Their kingdoms lost, and desolate
Their race sublime.

Who is the champion ? who the strong ?
Pontiff and priest, and sceptred throng ?
On these shall fall
As heavily the hand of Death,
As when it stays the shepherd's breath
Beside his stall.

I speak not of the Trojan name,
Neither its glory nor its shame
Has met our eyes ;
Nor of Rome's great and glorious dead,
Though we have heard so oft, and read,
Their histories.

Little avails it now to know
Of ages passed so long ago,
Nor how they rolled ;
Our theme shall be of yesterday,
Which to oblivion sweeps away,
Like days of old.

Where is the King, Don Juan ?   Where
Each royal prince and noble heir
Of Aragon ?
Where are the courtly gallantries ?
The deeds of love and high emprise,
In battle done ?

Tourney and joust, that charmed the eye,
And scarf, and gorgeous panoply,
And nodding plume, —
What were they but a pageant scene ?
What but the garlands, gay and green,
That deck the tomb ?

Where are the high-born dames, and where
Their gay attire, and jewelled hair,
And odors sweet ?
Where are the gentle knights, that came
To kneel, and breathe love's ardent flame,
Low at their feet ?

Where is the song of Troubadour ?
Where are the lute and gay tambour
They loved of yore ?
Where is the mazy dance of old,
The flowing robes, inwrought with gold,
The dancers wore ?

And he who next the sceptre swayed,
Henry, whose royal court displayed
Such power and pride ;
O, in what winning smiles arrayed,
The world its various pleasures laid
His throne beside !

But O ! how false and full of guile
That world, which wore so soft a smile
But to betray !
She, that had been his friend before,
Now from the fated monarch tore
Her charms away.

The countless gifts, — the stately walls,
The royal palaces, and halls
All filled with gold ;
Plate with armorial bearings wrought,
Chambers with ample treasures fraught
Of wealth untold ;

The noble steeds, and harness bright,
And gallant lord, and stalwart knight,
In rich array, —
Where shall we seek them now ? Alas !
Like the bright dewdrops on the grass,
They passed away.

His brother, too, whose factious zeal
Usurped the sceptre of Castile,
Unskilled to reign ;
What a gay, brilliant court had he,
When all the flower of chivalry
Was in his train !

But he was mortal ; and the breath,
That flamed from the hot forge of Death,
Blasted his years ;
Judgment of God ! that flame by thee,
When raging fierce and fearfully,
Was quenched in tears !

Spain's haughty Constable, — the true
And gallant Master, whom we knew
Most loved of all.
Breathe not a whisper of his pride, —
He on the gloomy scaffold died,
Ignoble fall !

The countless treasures of his care,
His hamlets green, and cities fair,
His mighty power, —
What were they all but grief and shame,
Tears and a broken heart, when came
The parting hour ?

His other brothers, proud and high,
Masters, who, in prosperity,
Might rival kings ;
Who made the bravest and the best
The bondsmen of their high behest,
Their underlings ;

What was their prosperous estate,
When high exalted and elate
With power and pride ?
What, but a transient gleam of light,
A flame, which, glaring at its height,
Grew dim and died ?

So many a duke of royal name,
Marquis and count of spotless fame,
And baron brave,
That might the sword of empire wield,
All these, O Death, hast thou concealed
In the dark grave !

Their deeds of mercy and of arms,
In peaceful days, or war's alarms,
When thou dost show,
O Death, thy stern and angry face,
One stroke of thy all-powerful mace
Can overthrow.

Unnumbered hosts, that threaten nigh,
Pennon and standard flaunting high,
And flag displayed ;
High battlements intrenched around,
Bastion, and moated wall, and mound,
And palisade,

And covered trench, secure and deep, —
All these cannot one victim keep,
O Death, from thee,
When thou dost battle in thy wrath,
And thy strong shafts pursue their path
Unerringly.

O World! so few the years we live,
Would that the life which thou dost give
Were life indeed!
Alas! thy sorrows fall so fast,
Our happiest hour is when at last
The soul is freed.

Our days are covered o'er with grief,
And sorrows neither few nor brief
Veil all in gloom;
Left desolate of real good,
Within this cheerless solitude
No pleasures bloom.

Thy pilgrimage begins in tears,
And ends in bitter doubts and fears,
Or dark despair ;
Midway so many toils appear,
That he who lingers longest here
Knows most of care.

Thy goods are bought with many a groan,
By the hot sweat of toil alone,
And weary hearts ;
Fleet-footed is the approach of woe,
But with a lingering step and slow
Its form departs.

And he, the good man's shield and shade,
To whom all hearts their homage paid,
As Virtue's son, —
Roderic Manrique, — he whose name
Is written on the scroll of Fame,
Spain's champion ;

His signal deeds and prowess high
Demand no pompous eulogy,—
Ye saw his deeds !
Why should their praise in verse be sung ?
The name, that dwells on every tongue,
No minstrel needs.

To friends a friend ; — how kind to all
The vassals of this ancient hall
And feudal fief !
To foes how stern a foe was he !
And to the valiant and the free
How brave a chief !

What prudence with the old and wise ;
What grace in youthful gayeties ;
In all how sage !
Benignant to the serf and slave,
He showed the base and falsely brave
A lion's rage.

His was Octavian's prosperous star,
The rush of Cæsar's conquering car
At battle's call ;
His, Scipio's virtue ; his, the skill
And the indomitable will
Of Hannibal.

His was a Trajan's goodness, — his
A Titus' noble charities
And righteous laws ;
The arm of Hector, and the might
Of Tully, to maintain the right
In truth's just cause ;

The clemency of Antonine,
Aurelius' countenance divine,
Firm, gentle, still ;
The eloquence of Adrian,
And Theodosius' love to man,
And generous will ;

In tented field and bloody fray,
An Alexander's vigorous sway
And stern command ;
The faith of Constantine ; ay, more,
The fervent love Camillus bore
His native land.

He left no well-filled treasury,
He heaped no pile of riches high,
Nor massive plate ;
He fought the Moors, — and, in their fall,
City and tower and castled wall
Were his estate.

Upon the hard-fought battle-ground,
Brave steeds and gallant riders found
A common grave ;
And there the warrior's hand did gain
The rents, and the long vassal train,
That conquest gave.

And if, of old, his halls displayed
The honored and exalted grade
His worth had gained,
So, in the dark, disastrous hour,
Brothers and bondsmen of his power
His hand sustained.

After high deeds, not left untold,
In the stern warfare, which of old
'T was his to share,
Such noble leagues he made, that more
And fairer regions, than before,
His guerdon were.

These are the records, half effaced,
Which, with the hand of youth, he traced
On history's page ;
But with fresh victories he drew
Each fading character anew
In his old age.

By his unrivalled skill, by great
And veteran service to the state,
By worth adored,
He stood, in his high dignity,
The proudest knight of chivalry,
Knight of the Sword.

He found his cities and domains
Beneath a tyrant's galling chains
And cruel power;
But, by fierce battle and blockade,
Soon his own banner was displayed
From every tower.

By the tried valor of his hand,
His monarch and his native land
Were nobly served; —
Let Portugal repeat the story,
And proud Castile, who shared the glory
His arms deserved.

And when so oft, for weal or woe,
His life upon the fatal throw
Had been cast down ;
When he had served, with patriot zeal,
Beneath the banner of Castile,
His sovereign's crown ;

And done such deeds of valor strong,
That neither history nor song
Can count them all ;
Then, on Ocaña's castled rock,
Death at his portal came to knock,
With sudden call, —

Saying, " Good Cavalier, prepare
To leave this world of toil and care
With joyful mien ;
Let thy strong heart of steel this day
Put on its armour for the fray, —
The closing scene.

" Since thou hast been, in battle-strife,
  So prodigal of health and life,
    For earthly fame,
  Let virtue nerve thy heart again ;
  Loud on the last stern battle-plain
    They call thy name.

" Think not the struggle that draws near
  Too terrible for man, — nor fear
    To meet the foe ;
  Nor let thy noble spirit grieve,
  Its life of glorious fame to leave
    On earth below.

" A life of honor and of worth
  Has no eternity on earth, —
    'T is but a name ;
  And yet its glory far exceeds
  That base and sensual life, which leads
    To want and shame.

" The eternal life, beyond the sky,
   Wealth cannot purchase, nor the high
   And proud estate ;
   The soul in dalliance laid, — the spirit
   Corrupt with sin, — shall not inherit
   A joy so great.

" But the good monk, in cloistered cell,
   Shall gain it by his book and bell,
   His prayers and tears ;
   And the brave knight, whose arm endures
   Fierce battle, and against the Moors
   His standard rears.

" And thou, brave knight, whose hand has poured
   The life-blood of the Pagan horde
   O'er all the land,
   In heaven shalt thou receive, at length,
   The guerdon of thine earthly strength
   And dauntless hand.

"Cheered onward by this promise sure,
Strong in the faith entire and pure
Thou dost profess,
Depart, — thy hope is certainty, —
The third — the better life on high
Shalt thou possess."

" O Death, no more, no more delay ;
My spirit longs to flee away,
And be at rest ;
The will of Heaven my will shall be, —
I bow to the divine decree,
To God's behest.

" My soul is ready to depart,
No thought rebels, the obedient heart
Breathes forth no sigh ;
The wish on earth to linger still
Were vain, when 't is God's sovereign will
That we shall die.

" O thou, that for our sins didst take
A human form, and humbly make
Thy home on earth ;
Thou, that to thy divinity
A human nature didst ally
By mortal birth,

" And in that form didst suffer here
Torment, and agony, and fear,
So patiently ;
By thy redeeming grace alone,
And not for merits of my own,
O, pardon me ! "

As thus the dying warrior prayed,
Without one gathering mist or shade
Upon his mind ;
Encircled by his family,
Watched by affection's gentle eye
So soft and kind ;

His soul to Him, who gave it, rose ;
God lead it to its long repose,
Its glorious rest!
And, though the warrior's sun has set,
Its light shall linger round us yet,
Bright, radiant, blest.*

---

* This poem of Manrique is a great favorite in Spain.
No less than four poetic Glosses, or running commentaries,
upon it have been published, no one of which, however,
possesses great poetic merit.   That of the Carthusian monk,
Rodrigo de Valdepeñas, is the best.   It is known as the
Glosa del Cartujo.   There is also a prose Commentary by
Luis de Aranda.

The following stanzas of the poem were found in 'he
author's pocket, after his death on the field of battle.

    " O World ! so few the years we live,
      Would that the life which thou dost give
      Were life indeed !
      Alas ! thy sorrows fall so fast,
      Our happiest hour is when at last
      The soul is freed.

" Our days are covered o'er with grief,
   And sorrows neither few nor brief
   Veil all in gloom;
   Left desolate of real good,
   Within this cheerless solitude
   No pleasures bloom.

" Thy pilgrimage begins in tears,
   And ends in bitter doubts and fears,
   Or dark despair;
   Midway so many toils appear,
   That he who lingers longest here
   Knows most of care.

" Thy goods are bought with many a groan,
   By the hot sweat of toil alone,
   And weary hearts;
   Fleet-footed is the approach of woe,
   But with a lingering step and slow
   Its form departs."

THE GOOD SHEPHERD.

FROM THE SPANISH OF LOPE DE VEGA.

SHEPHERD ! that with thine amorous, sylvan song
Hast broken the slumber which encompassed me,—
That mad'st thy crook from the accursed tree,
On which thy powerful arms were stretched so long!
Lead me to mercy's ever-flowing fountains ;
For thou my shepherd, guard, and guide shalt be;
I will obey thy voice, and wait to see
Thy feet all beautiful upon the mountains.

Hear, Shepherd!—thou who for thy flock art dying,

O, wash away these scarlet sins, for thou

Rejoicest at the contrite sinner's vow.

O, wait!—to thee my weary soul is crying,—

Wait for me!—Yet why ask it, when I see,

With feet nailed to the cross, thou 'rt waiting still

      for me!

TO-MORROW.

FROM THE SPANISH OF LOPE DE VEGA.

LORD, what am I, that, with unceasing care,
Thou didst seek after me, — that thou didst wait,
Wet with unhealthy dews, before my gate,
And pass the gloomy nights of winter there?
O strange delusion! — that I did not greet
Thy blest approach, and O, to Heaven how lost,
If my ingratitude's unkindly frost
Has chilled the bleeding wounds upon thy feet.

How oft my guardian angel gently cried,
" Soul, from thy casement look, and thou shalt see
How he persists to knock and wait for thee ! "
And, O ! how often to that voice of sorrow,
" To-morrow we will open," I replied,
And when the morrow came I answered still, " To-
          morrow."

THE NATIVE LAND.

FROM THE SPANISH OF FRANCISCO DE ALDANA.

CLEAR fount of light ! my native land on high,
Bright with a glory that shall never fade !
Mansion of truth ! without a veil or shade,
Thy holy quiet meets the spirit's eye.
There dwells the soul in its ethereal essence,
Gasping no longer for life's feeble breath ;
But, sentineled in heaven, its glorious presence
With pitying eye beholds, yet fears not, death.

Beloved country ! banished from thy shore,
A stranger in this prison-house of clay,
The exiled spirit weeps and sighs for thee !
Heavenward the bright perfections I adore
Direct, and the sure promise cheers the way,
That, whither love aspires, there shall my dwelling
    be.

THE IMAGE OF GOD.

FROM THE SPANISH OF FRANCISCO DE ALDANA.

O Lord! that seest, from yon starry height,
Centred in one the future and the past,
Fashioned in thine own image, see how fast
The world obscures in me what once was bright!
Eternal Sun! the warmth which thou hast given,
To cheer life's flowery April, fast decays;
Yet, in the hoary winter of my days,
For ever green shall be my trust in Heaven.

Celestial King ! O let thy presence pass
Before my spirit, and an image fair
Shall meet that look of mercy from on high,
As the reflected image in a glass
Doth meet the look of him who seeks it there,
And owes its being to the gazer's eye.

THE BROOK.

FROM THE SPANISH.

LAUGH of the mountain ! — lyre of bird and tree !
Pomp of the meadow ! mirror of the morn !
The soul of April, unto whom are born
The rose and jessamine, leaps wild in thee !
Although, where'er thy devious current strays,
The lap of earth with gold and silver teems,
To me thy clear proceeding brighter seems
Than golden sands, that charm each shepherd's
    gaze.

How without guile thy bosom, all transparent
As the pure crystal, lets the curious eye
Thy secrets scan, thy smooth, round pebbles count!
How, without malice murmuring, glides thy current!
O sweet simplicity of days gone by!
Thou shun'st the haunts of man, to dwell in lim-
    pid fount!

THE CELESTIAL PILOT.

FROM DANTE. PURGATORIO, II.

AND now, behold! as at the approach of morning,
Through the gross vapors, Mars grows fiery red
Down in the west upon the ocean floor,

Appeared to me,— may I again behold it !—
A light along the sea, so swiftly coming,
Its motion by no flight of wing is equalled.

And when therefrom I had withdrawn a little
Mine eyes, that I might question my conductor,
Again I saw it brighter grown and larger.

Thereafter, on all sides of it, appeared
I knew not what of white, and underneath,
Little by little, there came forth another.

My master yet had uttered not a word,
While the first brightness into wings unfolded ;
But, when he clearly recognised the pilot,

He cried aloud ; " Quick, quick, and bow the knee !
Behold the Angel of God ! fold up thy hands !
Henceforward shalt thou see such officers !

" See, how he scorns all human arguments,
So that no oar he wants, nor other sail
Than his own wings, between so distant shores !

" See, how he holds them, pointed straight to
       heaven,
Fanning the air with the eternal pinions,
That do not moult themselves like mortal hair ! "

And then, as nearer and more near us came
The Bird of Heaven, more glorious he appeared,
So that the eye could not sustain his presence,

But down I cast it ; and he came to shore
With a small vessel, gliding swift and light,
So that the water swallowed nought thereof.

Upon the stern stood the Celestial Pilot !
Beatitude seemed written in his face !
And more than a hundred spirits sat within.

" *In exitu Israel* out of Egypt ! "
Thus sang they all together in one voice,
With whatso in that Psalm is after written.

Then made he sign of holy rood upon them,
Whereat all cast themselves upon the shore,
And he departed swiftly as he came.

THE TERRESTRIAL PARADISE.

FROM DANTE. PURGATORIO, XXVIII.

Longing already to search in and round
The heavenly forest, dense and living-green,
Which to the eyes tempered the new-born day,

Withouten more delay I left the bank,
Crossing the level country slowly, slowly,
Over the soil, that everywhere breathed fragrance.

A gently-breathing air, that no mutation
Had in itself, smote me upon the forehead,
No heavier blow, than of a pleasant breeze,

Whereat the tremulous branches readily
Did all of them bow downward towards that side
Where its first shadow casts the Holy Mountain;

Yet not from their upright direction bent
So that the little birds upon their tops
Should cease the practice of their tuneful art;

But, with full-throated joy, the hours of prime
Singing received they in the midst of foliage
That made monotonous burden to their rhymes,

Even as from branch to branch it gathering swells,
Through the pine forests on the shore of Chiassi,
When Æolus unlooses the Sirocco.

Already my slow steps had led me on
Into the ancient wood so far, that I
Could see no more the place where I had entered.

And lo! my farther course cut off a river,
Which, towards the left hand, with its little waves,
Bent down the grass, that on its margin sprang.

All waters that on earth most limpid are,
Would seem to have within themselves some mix-
      ture,
Compared with that, which nothing doth conceal,

Although it moves on with a brown, brown current,
Under the shade perpetual, that never
Ray of the sun lets in, nor of the moon.

BEATRICE.

FROM DANTE.   PURGATORIO, XXX., XXXI.

EVEN as the Blessed, in the new covenant,
Shall rise up quickened, each one from his grave,
Wearing again the garments of the flesh,

So, upon that celestial chariot,
A hundred rose *ad vocem tanti senis*,
Ministers and messengers of life eternal.

They all were saying ; " *Benedictus qui venis*,"
And scattering flowers above and round about,
" *Manibus o date lilia plenis*."

I once beheld, at the approach of day,
The orient sky all stained with roseate hues,
And the other heaven with light serene adorned,

And the sun's face uprising, overshadowed,
So that, by temperate influence of vapors,
The eye sustained his aspect for long while ;

Thus in the bosom of a cloud of flowers,
Which from those hands angelic were thrown up,
And down descended inside and without,

With crown of olive o'er a snow-white veil,
Appeared a lady, under a green mantle,
Vested in colors of the living flame.

*   *   *   *   *

Even as the snow, among the living rafters
Upon the back of Italy, congeals,
Blown on and beaten by Sclavonian winds,

And then, dissolving, filters through itself,
Whene'er the land, that loses shadow, breathes,
Like as a taper melts before a fire,

Even such I was, without a sigh or tear,
Before the song of those who chime for ever
After the chiming of the eternal spheres ;

But, when I heard in those sweet melodies
Compassion for me, more than had they said,
"O wherefore, lady, dost thou thus consume him?"

The ice, that was about my heart congealed,
To air and water changed, and, in my anguish,
Through lips and eyes came gushing from my
        breast.

*   *   *   *   *

Confusion and dismay, together mingled,
Forced such a feeble " Yes ! " out of my mouth,
To understand it one had need of sight.

Even as a cross-bow breaks, when 't is discharged,
Too tensely drawn the bow-string and the bow,
And with less force the arrow hits the mark ;

So I gave way under this heavy burden,
Gushing forth into bitter tears and sighs,
And the voice, fainting, flagged upon its passage.

SPRING.

FROM THE FRENCH OF CHARLES D'ORLEANS.

XV. CENTURY.

GENTLE Spring ! — in sunshine clad,
  Well dost thou thy power display !
For Winter maketh the light heart sad,
  And thou, — thou makest the sad heart gay.
He sees thee, and calls to his gloomy train,
The sleet, and the snow, and the wind, and the rain ;
And they shrink away, and they flee in fear,
  When thy merry step draws near.

Winter giveth the fields and the trees, so old,
    Their beards of icicles and snow ;
And the rain, it raineth so fast and cold,
    We must cower over the embers low ;
And, snugly housed from the wind and weather,
Mope like birds that are changing feather.
But the storm retires, and the sky grows clear,
    When thy merry step draws near.

Winter maketh the sun in the gloomy sky
    Wrap him round with a mantle of cloud ;
But, Heaven be praised, thy step is nigh ;
    Thou tearest away the mournful shroud,
And the earth looks bright, and Winter surly,
Who has toiled for nought both late and early,
Is banished afar by the new-born year,
    When thy merry step draws near.

THE CHILD ASLEEP.

FROM THE FRENCH.

Sweet babe! true portrait of thy father's face,
   Sleep on the bosom, that thy lips have pressed!
Sleep, little one; and closely, gently place
   Thy drowsy eyelid on thy mother's breast.

Upon that tender eye, my little friend,
   Soft sleep shall come, that cometh not to me!
I watch to see thee, nourish thee, defend; —
   'T is sweet to watch for thee, — alone for thee!

His arms fall down ; sleep sits upon his brow ;
  His eye is closed ; he sleeps, nor dreams of harm.
Wore not his cheek the apple's ruddy glow,
  Would you not say he slept on Death's cold arm?

Awake, my boy ! — I tremble with affright !
  Awake, and chase this fatal thought !—Unclose
Thine eye but for one moment on the light !
  Even at the price of thine, give me repose !

Sweet error!—he but slept,—I breathe again;—
  Come, gentle dreams, the hour of sleep beguile!
O ! when shall he, for whom I sigh in vain,
  Beside me watch to see thy waking smile ?

THE GRAVE.

FROM THE ANGLO-SAXON

For thee was a house built
Ere thou wast born,
For thee was a mould meant
Ere thou of mother camest.
But it is not made ready,
Nor its depth measured,
Nor is it seen
How long it shall be.

8

Now I bring thee
Where thou shalt be ;
Now I shall measure thee,
And the mould afterwards

Thy house is not
Highly timbered,
It is unhigh and low ;
When thou art therein,
The heel-ways are low,
The side-ways unhigh.
The roof is built
Thy breast full nigh,
So thou shalt in mould
Dwell full cold,
Dimly and dark.

Doorless is that house,
And dark it is within ;

There thou art fast detained
And Death hath the key.
Loathsome is that earth-house,
And grim within to dwell.
There thou shalt dwell,
And worms shall divide thee.

   Thus thou art laid,
And leavest thy friends ;
Thou hast no friend,
Who will come to thee,
Who will ever see
How that house pleaseth thee ;
Who will ever open
The door for thee
And descend after thee,
For soon thou art loathsome
And hateful to see.

KING CHRISTIAN.

A NATIONAL SONG OF DENMARK.

FROM THE DANISH OF JOHANNES EVALD.

KING CHRISTIAN stood by the lofty mast
    In mist and smoke ;
His sword was hammering so fast,
Through Gothic helm and brain it passed ;
Then sank each hostile hulk and mast,
    In mist and smoke.
" Fly ! " shouted they, " fly, he who can !
Who braves of Denmark's Christian
    The stroke ? "

Nils Juel gave heed to the tempest's roar,
    Now is the hour !
He hoisted his blood-red flag once more,
And smote upon the foe full sore,
And shouted loud, through the tempest's roar,
    " Now is the hour ! "
" Fly ! " shouted they, " for shelter fly !
Of Denmark's Juel who can defy
    The power ? "

North Sea ! a glimpse of Wessel rent
    Thy murky sky !
Then champions to thine arms were sent ;
Terror and Death glared where he went ;
From the waves was heard a wail, that rent
    Thy murky sky !
From Denmark, thunders Tordenskiol ',
Let each to Heaven commend his soul,
    And fly !

Path of the Dane to fame and might !
    Dark-rolling wave !
Receive thy friend, who, scorning flight,
Goes to meet danger with despite,
Proudly as thou the tempest's might,
    Dark-rolling wave !
And amid pleasures and alarms,
And war and victory, be thine arms
    My grave ! *

* Nils Juel was a celebrated Danish Admiral, and Peder
Wessel, a Vice-Admiral, who for his great prowess received
the popular title of Tordenskiold, or *Thunder-shield.* In
childhood he was a tailor's apprentice, and rose to his high
rank before the age of twenty-eight, when he was killed in
a duel.

THE HAPPIEST LAND.

FRAGMENT OF A MODERN BALLAD.

FROM THE GERMAN.

THERE sat one day in quiet,
　　By an alehouse on the Rhine,
Four hale and hearty fellows,
　　And drank the precious wine.

The landlord's daughter filled their cups,
　　Around the rustic board ;
Then sat they all so calm and still,
　　And spake not one rude word.

But, when the maid departed,
    A Swabian raised his hand,
And cried, all hot and flushed with wine,
    " Long live the Swabian land !

" The greatest kingdom upon earth
    Cannot with that compare ;
With all the stout and hardy men
    And the nut-brown maidens there."

" Ha ! " cried a Saxon, laughing, —
    And dashed his beard with wine ;
" I had rather live in Lapland,
    Than that Swabian land of thine !

" The goodliest land on all this earth,
    It is the Saxon land !
There have I as many maidens
    As fingers on this hand ! "

" Hold your tongues! both Swabian and Saxon!"
   A bold Bohemian cries ;
" If there 's a heaven upon this earth,
   In Bohemia it lies.

" There the tailor blows the flute,
   And the cobler blows the horn,
And the miner blows the bugle,
   Over mountain gorge and bourn."

     *   *   *   *   *

And then the landlord's daughter
   Up to heaven raised her hand,
And said, " Ye may no more contend,—
   There lies the happiest land ! "

THE WAVE.

FROM THE GERMAN OF TIEDGE.

" WHITHER, thou turbid wave ?
Whither, with so much haste,
As if a thief wert thou ? "

" I am the Wave of Life,
Stained with my margin's dust ;
From the struggle and the strife
Of the narrow stream I fly
To the Sea's immensity,
To wash from me the slime
Of the muddy banks of Time."

THE DEAD.

FROM THE GERMAN OF KLOPSTOCK.

How they so softly rest,
All, all the holy dead,
Unto whose dwelling-place
Now doth my soul draw near!
How they so softly rest,
All in their silent graves,
Deep to corruption
Slowly down-sinking!

And they no longer weep,
Here, where complaint is still!
And they no longer feel,
Here, where all gladness flies!
And, by the cypresses
Softly o'ershadowed,
Until the Angel
Calls them, they slumber!

THE BIRD AND THE SHIP.

FROM THE GERMAN OF MÜLLER.

" THE rivers rush into the sea,
　　By castle and town they go ;
The winds behind them merrily
　　Their noisy trumpets blow.

" The clouds are passing far and high,
　　We little birds in them play ;
And every thing, that can sing and fly,
　　Goes with us, and far away.

"I greet thee, bonny boat! Whither, or whence,
　With thy fluttering golden band?"—
"I greet thee, little bird! To the wide sea
　I haste from the narrow land.

"Full and swollen is every sail;
　I see no longer a hill,
I have trusted all to the sounding gale,
　And it will not let me stand still.

"And wilt thou, little bird, go with us?
　Thou mayest stand on the mainmast tall,
For full to sinking is my house
　With merry companions all."—

"I need not and seek not company,
　Bonny boat, I can sing all alone;
For the mainmast tall too heavy am I,
　Bonny boat, I have wings of my own.

" High over the sails, high over the mast,
  Who shall gainsay these joys ?
When thy merry companions are still, at last,
  Thou shalt hear the sound of my voice.

" Who neither may rest, nor listen may,
  God bless them every one !
I dart away, in the bright blue day,
  And the golden fields of the sun.

" Thus do I sing my weary song,
  Wherever the four winds blow ;
And this same song, my whole life long,
  Neither Poet nor Printer may know."

WHITHER?

FROM THE GERMAN OF MÜLLER.

I HEARD a brooklet gushing
   From its rocky fountain near,
Down into the valley rushing,
   So fresh and wondrous clear.

I know not what came o'er me,
   Nor who the counsel gave ;
But I must hasten downward,
   All with mv pilgrim-stave ;

Downward, and ever farther,
   And ever the brook beside ;
And ever fresher murmured,
   And ever clearer, the tide.

Is this the way I was going ?
   Whither, O brooklet, say !
Thou hast, with thy soft murmur,
   Murmured my senses away.

What do I say of a murmur ?
   That can no murmur be ;
'T is the water-nymphs, that are singing
   Their roundelays under me.

Let them sing, my friend, let them murmur,
   And wander merrily near ;
The wheels of a mill are going
   In every brooklet clear.

9

BEWARE!

FROM THE GERMAN.

I KNOW a maiden fair to see,
　　Take care !
She can both false and friendly be,
　　Beware !　Beware !
　　Trust her not,
She is fooling thee !

She has two eyes, so soft and brown,
　　Take care !
She gives a side-glance and looks down,
　　Beware !　Beware !
　　Trust her not,
She is fooling thee !

And she has hair of a golden hue,
    Take care!
And what she says, it is not true,
    Beware!   Beware!
    Trust her not,
She is fooling thee!

She has a bosom as white as snow,
    Take care!
She knows how much it is best to show,
    Beware!   Beware!
    Trust her not,
She is fooling thee!

She gives thee a garland woven fair,
    Take care!
It is a fool's-cap for thee to wear,
    Beware! Beware!
    Trust her not,
She is fooling thee!

SONG OF THE BELL.

FROM THE GERMAN.

BELL ! thou soundest merrily,
When the bridal party
   To the church doth hie !
Bell ! thou soundest solemnly,
When, on Sabbath morning,
   Fields deserted lie !

Bell ! thou soundest merrily ;
Tellest thou at evening,
   Bed-time draweth nigh !
Bell ! thou soundest mournfully
Tellest thou the bitter
   Parting hath gone by !

Say! how canst thou mourn?
How canst thou rejoice?
　　Thou art but metal dull!
And yet all our sorrowings,
And all our rejoicings,
　　Thou dost feel them all!

God hath wonders many,
Which we cannot fathom,
　　Placed within thy form!
When the heart is sinking,
Thou alone canst raise it,
　　Trembling in the storm!

THE CASTLE BY THE SEA.

FROM THE GERMAN OF UHLAND.

" HAST thou seen that lordly castle,
  That Castle by the Sea ?
Golden and red above it
  The clouds float gorgeously.

" And fain it would stoop downward
  To the mirrored wave below ;
And fain it would soar upward
  In the evening's crimson glow."

" Well have I seen that castle,
　　That Castle by the Sea,
And the moon above it standing,
　　And the mist rise solemnly."

" The winds and the waves of ocean,
　　Had they a merry chime ?
Didst thou hear, from those lofty chambers,
　　The harp and the minstrel's rhyme ? "

" The winds and the waves of ocean,
　　They rested quietly,
But I heard on the gale a sound of wail,
　　And tears came to mine eye."

" And sawest thou on the turrets
　　The King and his royal bride ?
And the wave of their crimson mantles ?
　　And the golden crown of pride ?

" Led they not forth, in rapture,
   A beauteous maiden there ?
Resplendent as the morning sun,
   Beaming with golden hair ? "

" Well saw I the ancient parents,
   Without the crown of pride ;
They were moving slow, in weeds of woe,
   No maiden was by their side ! "

THE BLACK KNIGHT.

FROM THE GERMAN OF UHLAND.

'T was Pentecost, the Feast of Gladness,
When woods and fields put off all sadness.
  Thus began the King and spake ;
" So from the halls
Of ancient Hofburg's walls,
  A luxuriant Spring shall break."

Drums and trumpets echo loudly,
Wave the crimson banners proudly.
  From balcony the King looked on ;
In the play of spears,
Fell all the cavaliers,
  Before the monarch's stalwart son.

To the barrier of the fight
Rode at last a sable Knight.
    " Sir Knight! your name and scutcheon, say!"
" Should I speak it here,
Ye would stand aghast with fear ;
    I am a Prince of mighty sway ! "

When he rode into the lists,
The arch of heaven grew black with mists,
    And the castle 'gan to rock.
At the first blow,
Fell the youth from saddle-bow,
    Hardly rises from the shock.

Pipe and viol call the dances,
Torch-light through the high halls glances ;
    Waves a mighty shadow in ;
With manner bland
Doth ask the maiden's hand,
    Doth with her the dance begin ;

Danced in sable iron sark,
Danced a measure weird and dark,
  Coldly clasped her limbs around.
From breast and hair
Down fall from her the fair
  Flowerets, faded, to the ground.

To the sumptuous banquet came
Every Knight and every Dame.
  'Twixt son and daughter all distraught,
With mournful mind
The ancient King reclined,
  Gazed at them in silent thought.

Pale the children both did look,
But the guest a beaker took ;
  " Golden wine will make you whole ! "
The children drank,
Gave many a courteous thank ;
  " O that draught was very cool ! "

Each the father's breast embraces,
Son and daughter; and their faces
   Colorless grow utterly.
Whichever way
Looks the fear-struck father gray,
   He beholds his children die.

"Woe! the blessed children both
Takest thou in the joy of youth;
   Take me, too, the joyless father!
Spake the grim Guest,
From his hollow, cavernous breast,
   "Roses in the spring I gather!"

SONG OF THE SILENT LAND.

FROM THE GERMAN OF SALIS.

Into the Silent Land!
Ah! who shall lead us thither?
Clouds in the evening sky more darkly gather,
And shattered wrecks lie thicker on the strand.
Who leads us with a gentle hand
Thither, O thither,
Into the Silent Land?

Into the Silent Land!
To you, ye boundless regions
Of all perfection! Tender morning-visions

Of beauteous souls! The Future's pledge and band!
Who in Life's battle firm doth stand,
Shall bear Hope's tender blossoms
Into the Silent Land!

O Land! O Land!
For all the broken-hearted
The mildest herald by our fate allotted,
Beckons, and with inverted torch doth stand
To lead us with a gentle hand
Into the land of the great Departed,
Into the Silent Land!

L'ENVOI.

———

Ye voices, that arose
After the Evening's close,
And whispered to my restless heart repose!

Go, breathe it in the ear
Of all who doubt and fear,
And say to them, " Be of good cheer ! "

———

Ye sounds, so low and calm,
That in the groves of balm
Seemed to me like an angel's psalm !

Go, mingle yet once more
With the perpetual roar
Of the pine forest, dark and hoar!

Tongues of the dead, not lost,
But speaking from death's frost,
Like fiery tongues at Pentecost!

Glimmer, as funeral lamps,
Amid the chills and damps
Of the vast plain where Death encamps!

BALLADS

AND

OTHER POEMS.

1842.

10

PREFACE.

——

THERE is one poem in this volume, in reference to which a few introductory remarks may be useful. It is *The Children of the Lord's Supper*, from the Swedish of Bishop Tegnér; a poem which enjoys no inconsiderable reputation in the North of Europe, and for its beauty and simplicity merits the attention of English readers. It is an Idyl, descriptive of scenes in a Swedish village; and belongs to the same class of poems, as the *Luise* of Voss and the *Hermann und Dorothea* of Göthe. But the Swedish Poet has been

guided by a surer taste, than his German pre-
decessors. His tone is pure and elevated;
and he rarely, if ever, mistakes what is trivial
for what is simple.

There is something patriarchal still linger-
ing about rural life in Sweden, which renders
it a fit theme for song. Almost primeval sim-
plicity reigns over that Northern land, — al-
most primeval solitude and stillness. You
pass out from the gate of the city, and, as if
by magic, the scene changes to a wild, wood-
land landscape. Around you are forests of fir.
Over head hang the long, fan-like branches,
trailing with moss, and heavy with red and
blue cones. Under foot is a carpet of yellow
leaves; and the air is warm and balmy. On
a wooden bridge you cross a little silver
stream; and anon come forth into a pleasant
and sunny land of farms. Wooden fences

divide the adjoining fields. Across the road
are gates, which are opened by troops of chil-
dren. The peasants take off their hats as you
pass; you sneeze, and they cry, "God bless
you." The houses in the villages and small-
er towns are all built of hewn timber, and for
the most part painted red. The floors of the
taverns are strewn with the fragrant tips of
fir boughs. In many villages there are no
taverns, and the peasants take turns in receiv-
ing travellers. The thrifty housewife shows
you into the best chamber, the walls of which
are hung round with rude pictures from the
Bible; and brings you her heavy silver spoons,
— an heirloom, — to dip the curdled milk from
the pan. You have oaten cakes baked some
months before; or bread with anise-seed and
coriander in it, or perhaps a little pine bark.

Meanwhile the sturdy husband has brought

his horses from the plough, and harnessed
them to your carriage.   Solitary travellers
come and go in uncouth one-horse chaises.
Most of them have pipes in their mouths, and
hanging around their necks in front, a leather
wallet, in which they carry tobacco, and the
great bank notes of the country, as large as
your two hands.   You meet, also, groups of
Dalekarlian peasant women, travelling home-
ward or town-ward in pursuit of work.   They
walk barefoot, carrying in their hands their
shoes, which have high heels under the hol-
low of the foot, and soles of birch bark.

Frequent, too, are the village churches,
standing by the road-side, each in its own
little garden of Gethsemane.   In the parish
register great events are doubtless recorded.
Some old king was christened or buried in
that church ; and a little sexton, with a rusty

key, shows you the baptismal font, or the coffin. In the church-yard are a few flowers, and much green grass; and daily the shadow of the church spire, with its long tapering finger, counts the tombs, representing a dial-plate of human life, on which the hours and minutes are the graves of men. The stones are flat, and large, and low, and perhaps sunken, like the roofs of old houses. On some are armorial bearings; on others only the initials of the poor tenants, with a date, as on the roofs of Dutch cottages. They all sleep with their heads to the westward. Each held a lighted taper in his hand when he died; and in his coffin were placed his little heart-treasures, and a piece of money for his last journey. Babes that came lifeless into the world were carried in the arms of gray-haired old men to the only cradle they ever slept in;

and in the shroud of the dead mother were
laid the little garments of the child, that lived
and died in her bosom. And over this scene
the village pastor looks from his window in
the stillness of midnight, and says in his
heart, "How quietly they rest, all the de-
parted!"

Near the church-yard gate stands a poor-
box, fastened to a post by iron bands, and
secured by a padlock, with a sloping wooden
roof to keep off the rain. If it be Sunday,
the peasants sit on the church steps and con
their psalm-books. Others are coming down
the road with their beloved pastor, who talks
to them of holy things from beneath his
broad-brimmed hat. He speaks of fields and
harvests, and of the parable of the sower, that
went forth to sow. He leads them to the
Good Shepherd, and to the pleasant pastures

of the spirit-land. He is their patriarch, and, like Melchizedek, both priest and king, though he has no other throne than the church pulpit. The women carry psalm-books in their hands, wrapped in silk handkerchiefs, and listen devoutly to the good man's words. But the young men, like Gallio, care for none of these things. They are busy counting the plaits in the kirtles of the peasant girls, their number being an indication of the wearer's wealth. It may end in a wedding.

I will endeavour to describe a village wedding in Sweden. It shall be in summer time, that there may be flowers, and in a southern province, that the bride may be fair. The early song of the lark and of chanticleer are mingling in the clear morning air, and the sun, the heavenly bridegroom with golden locks, arises in the east, just as our earthly bridegroom with yellow hair, arises in the south. In the yard there is a sound of voices and trampling of hoofs, and horses are led forth and saddled. The steed that is to bear the bridegroom has a bunch of flowers upon his forehead, and a garland of corn-flowers around his neck. Friends from the neighbouring farms come riding in, their blue cloaks streaming to the wind; and finally the happy bridegroom, with a whip in his hand, and a monstrous nosegay in the breast of his black jacket, comes forth from his chamber; and then to horse and away, towards the village where the bride already sits and waits.

Foremost rides the Spokesman, followed by some half dozen village musicians. Next comes the bridegroom between his two groomsmen, and then forty or fifty friends and wedding guests, half of them perhaps with pistols

and guns in their hands. A kind of baggage-
wagon brings up the rear, laden with food
and drink for these merry pilgrims. At the
entrance of every village stands a triumphal
arch, adorned with flowers and ribands and
evergreens; and as they pass beneath it the
wedding guests fire a salute, and the whole
procession stops. And straight from every
pocket flies a black-jack, filled with punch or
brandy. It is passed from hand to hand among
the crowd; provisions are brought from the
wagon, and after eating and drinking and hur-
rahing, the procession moves forward again, and
at length draws near the house of the bride.
Four heralds ride forward to announce that a
knight and his attendants are in the neigh-
bouring forest, and pray for hospitality. "How
many are you?" asks the bride's father. "At
least three hundred," is the answer; and to

this the host replies, " Yes; were you seven
times as many, you should all be welcome;
and in token thereof receive this cup." Where-
upon each herald receives a can of ale; and
soon after the whole jovial company comes
storming into the farmer's yard, and, riding
round the May-pole, which stands in the cen-
tre, alights amid a grand salute and flourish of
music.

In the hall sits the bride, with a crown up-
on her head and a tear in her eye, like the
Virgin Mary in old church paintings. She is
dressed in a red boddice and kirtle, with loose
linen sleeves. There is a gilded belt around
her waist; and around her neck strings of
golden beads, and a golden chain. On the
crown rests a wreath of wild roses, and below
it another of cypress. Loose over her shoul-
ders falls her flaxen hair; and her blue inno-

cent eyes are fixed upon the ground. O thou
good soul! thou hast hard hands, but a soft
heart! Thou art poor. The very ornaments
thou wearest are not thine. They have been
hired for this great day. Yet art thou rich;
rich in health, rich in hope, rich in thy first,
young, fervent love. The blessing of heaven
be upon thee! So thinks the parish priest, as
he joins together the hands of bride and bride-
groom, saying in deep, solemn tones, — " I
give thee in marriage this damsel, to be thy
wedded wife in all honor, and to share the
half of thy bed, thy lock and key, and every
third penny which you two may possess, or
may inherit, and all the rights which Upland's
laws provide, and the holy king Erik gave."

The dinner is now served, and the bride
sits between the bridegroom and the priest.
The Spokesman delivers an oration after the

ancient custom of his fathers. He interlards
it well with quotations from the Bible; and
invites the Saviour to be present at this mar-
riage feast, as he was at the marriage feast in
Cana of Galilee. The table is not sparingly
set forth. Each makes a long arm, and the
feast goes cheerly on. Punch and brandy pass
round between the courses, and here and there
a pipe is smoked, while waiting for the next
dish. They sit long at table; but, as all
things must have an end, so must a Swedish
dinner. Then the dance begins. It is led
off by the bride and the priest, who perform a
solemn minuet together. Not till after mid-
night comes the Last Dance. The girls form
a ring around the bride, to keep her from the
hands of the married women, who endeavour
to break through the magic circle, and seize
their new sister. After long struggling they

succeed; and the crown is taken from her
head and the jewels from her neck, and her
boddice is unlaced and her kirtle taken off;
and like a vestal virgin clad all in white she
goes, but it is to her marriage chamber, not to
her grave; and the wedding guests follow
her with lighted candles in their hands. And
this is a village bridal.

Nor must I forget the suddenly changing sea-
sons of the Northern clime. There is no long
and lingering spring, unfolding leaf and blos-
som one by one; — no long and lingering au-
tumn, pompous with many-colored leaves and
the glow of Indian summers. But winter
and summer are wonderful, and pass into each
other. The quail has hardly ceased piping
in the corn, when winter from the folds of
trailing clouds sows broad-cast over the land
snow, icicles, and rattling hail. The days

wane apace. Ere long the sun hardly rises
above the horizon, or does not rise at all.
The moon and the stars shine through the
day; only, at noon, they are pale and wan,
and in the southern sky a red, fiery glow, as
of sunset, burns along the horizon, and then
goes out. And pleasantly under the silver
moon, and under the silent, solemn stars, ring
the steel-shoes of the skaters on the frozen
sea, and voices, and the sound of bells.

And now the Northern Lights begin to
burn, faintly at first, like sunbeams playing
in the waters of the blue sea. Then a soft
crimson glow tinges the heavens. There is
a blush on the cheek of night. The colors
come and go; and change from crimson to
gold, from gold to crimson. The snow is
stained with rosy light. Twofold from the
zenith, east and west, flames a fiery sword;

and a broad band passes athwart the heavens, like a summer sunset. Soft purple clouds come sailing over the sky, and through their vapory folds the winking stars shine white as silver. With such pomp as this is Merry Christmas ushered in, though only a single star heralded the first Christmas. And in memory of that day the Swedish peasants dance on straw; and the peasant girls throw straws at the timbered roof of the hall, and for every one that sticks in a crack shall a groomsman come to their wedding. Merry Christmas indeed! For pious souls there shall be church songs and sermons, but for Swedish peasants, brandy and nut brown ale in wooden bowls; and the great Yulecake crowned with a cheese, and garlanded with apples, and upholding a three-armed candlestick over the Christmas feast. They may tell tales,

11

too, of Jöns Lundsbracka, and Lunkenfus, and
the great Riddar Finke of Pingsdaga.*

And now the glad, leafy mid-summer, full
of blossoms and the song of nightingales, is
come! Saint John has taken the flowers and
festival of heathen Balder; and in every vil-
lage there is a May-pole fifty feet high, with
wreaths and roses and ribands streaming in
the wind, and a noisy weathercock on top, to
tell the village whence the wind cometh and
whither it goeth. The sun does not set till
ten o'clock at night; and the children are at
play in the streets an hour later. The win-
dows and doors are all open, and you may sit
and read till midnight without a candle. O
how beautiful is the summer night, which is
not night, but a sunless yet unclouded day,
descending upon earth with dews, and shad-

* Titles of Swedish popular tales.

ows, and refreshing coolness! How beauti-
ful the long, mild twilight, which like a silver
clasp unites to-day with yesterday! How
beautiful the silent hour, when Morning and
Evening thus sit together, hand in hand, be-
neath the starless sky of midnight! From
the church-tower in the public square the bell
tolls the hour, with a soft, musical chime;
and the watchman, whose watch-tower is the
belfry, blows a blast in his horn, for each
stroke of the hammer, and four times, to the
four corners of the heavens, in a sonorous voice
he chaunts, —

> "Ho! watchman, ho!
> Twelve is the clock!
> God keep our town
> From fire and brand
> And hostile hand!
> Twelve is the clock!"

From his swallow's nest in the belfry he can
see the sun all night long; and farther north

the priest stands at his door in the warm mid-
night, and lights his pipe with a common
burning glass.

I trust that these remarks will not be deemed
irrelevant to the poem, but will lead to a clear-
er understanding of it. The translation is lit-
eral, perhaps to a fault. In no instance have
I done the author a wrong, by introducing
into his work any supposed improvements or
embellishments of my own. I have preserved
even the measure; that inexorable hexameter,
in which, it must be confessed, the motions
of the English Muse are not unlike those of
a prisoner dancing to the music of his chains;
and perhaps, as Dr. Johnson said of the dan-
cing dog, "the wonder is not that she should
do it so well, but that she should do it at all."

Esaias Tegnér, the author of this poem, was
born in the parish of By in Wärmland, in the

year 1782. In 1799 he entered the University of Lund, as a student; and in 1812 was appointed Professor of Greek in that institution. In 1824 he became Bishop of Wexiö, which office he still holds. He stands first among all the poets of Sweden, living or dead. His principal work is Frithiofs Saga; one of the most remarkable poems of the age. This modern Scald has written his name in immortal runes. He is the glory and boast of Sweden; a prophet, honored in his own country, and adding one more to the list of great names, that adorn her history.

1841.

BALLADS.

THE SKELETON IN ARMOUR.

[THE following Ballad was suggested to me while riding on the seashore at Newport. A year or two previous a skeleton had been dug up at Fall River, clad in broken and corroded armour; and the idea occurred to me of connecting it with the Round Tower at Newport, generally known hitherto as the Old Wind-Mill, though now claimed by the Danes as a work of their early ancestors. Professor Rafn, in the *Mémoires de la Société Royale des Antiquaires du Nord*, for 1838 – 1839, says;

" There is no mistaking in this instance the style in which the more ancient stone edifices of the North were constructed, the style which belongs to the Roman or Ante-Gothic architecture, and which, especially after the time of Charlemagne, diffused itself from Italy over the whole of the West and North of Europe, where it continued to predominate until the close of the 12th century; that style, which some authors have, from one of its most striking characteristics, called the round arch style, the same which in England is denominated Saxon and sometimes Norman architecture.

" On the ancient structure in Newport there are no ornaments remaining, which might possibly have served to guide us in assigning the probable date of its erection. That no vestige whatever is found of the pointed arch, nor any approximation to it, is indicative of an earlier rather than of a later period. From such characteristics as remain, however, we can scarcely form any other inference than one, in which I am persuaded that all, who are familiar with Old-Northern architecture, will concur, THAT THIS BUILDING WAS ERECTED AT A PERIOD DECIDEDLY NOT LATER THAN THE 12TH CENTURY. This remark applies, of course, to the original building only, and not to the alterations that it subsequently received; for there are several such alterations in the upper part of the building which cannot be mistaken, and which were most likely occasioned by its being adapted in modern times to various uses, for example as the substructure of a wind-mill, and latterly as a hay magazine. To the same times may be referred the windows, the fire-place, and the apertures made above the columns. That this building

could not have been erected for a wind-mill, is what an archi
tect will easily discern."

I will not enter into a discussion of the point. It is suffi-
ciently well established for the purpose of a ballad; though
doubtless many an honest citizen of Newport, who has
passed his days within sight of the Round Tower, will be
ready to exclaim with Sancho; " God bless me! did I not
warn you to have a care of what you were doing, for that
it was nothing but a wind-mill; and nobody could mistake it,
but one who had the like in his head.']

"SPEAK! speak! thou fearful guest!
  Who, with thy hollow breast
  Still in rude armour drest,
      Comest to daunt me!
  Wrapt not in Eastern balms,
  But with thy fleshless palms
  Stretched, as if asking alms,
      Why dost thou haunt me?"

Then, from those cavernous eyes
Pale flashes seemed to rise,
As when the Northern skies
  Gleam in December ;
And, like the water's flow
Under December's snow,
Came a dull voice of woe
  From the heart's chamber.

" I was a Viking old !
My deeds, though manifold,
No Skald in song has told,
  No Saga taught thee !
Take heed, that in thy verse
Thou dost the tale rehearse,
Else dread a dead man's curse !
  For this I sought thee.

" Far in the Northern Land,
    By the wild Baltic's strand,
    I, with my childish hand,
        Tamed the ger-falcon ;
    And, with my skates fast-bound,
    Skimmed the half-frozen Sound,
    That the poor whimpering hound
        Trembled to walk on.

" Oft to his frozen lair
    Tracked I the grisly bear,
    While from my path the hare
        Fled like a shadow ;
    Oft through the forest dark
    Followed the were-wolf's bark,
    Until the soaring lark
        Sang from the meadow.

" But when I older grew,
  Joining a corsair's crew,
  O'er the dark sea I flew
      With the marauders.
  Wild was the life we led ;
  Many the souls that sped,
  Many the hearts that bled,
      By our stern orders.

" Many a wassail-bout
  Wore the long Winter out ;
  Often our midnight shout
      Set the cocks crowing,
  As we the Berserk's tale
  Measured in cups of ale,
  Draining the oaken pail,
      Filled to o'erflowing.

" Once as I told in glee
　　Tales of the stormy sea,
　　Soft eyes did gaze on me,
　　　　Burning yet tender ;
　　And as the white stars shine
　　On the dark Norway pine,
　　On that dark heart of mine
　　　　Fell their soft splendor.

" I wooed the blue-eyed maid,
　　Yielding, yet half afraid,
　　And in the forest's shade
　　　　Our vows were plighted.
　　Under its loosened vest
　　Fluttered ·her little breast,
　　Like birds within their nest
　　　　By the hawk frighted.

" Bright in her father's hall
　　Shields gleamed upon the wall,
　　Loud sang the minstrels all,
　　　　Chaunting his glory;
　　When of old Hildebrand
　　I asked his daughter's hand,
　　Mute did the minstrels stand
　　　　To hear my story.

" While the brown ale he quaffed,
　　Loud then the champion laughed,
　　And as the wind-gusts waft
　　　　The sea-foam brightly,
　　So the loud laugh of scorn,
　　Out of those lips unshorn,
　　From the deep drinking-horn
　　　　Blew the foam lightly.

" She was a Prince's child,
  I but a Viking wild,
  And though she blushed and smiled,
      I was discarded !
  Should not the dove so white
  Follow the sea-mew's flight,
  Why did they leave that night
      Her nest unguarded ?

" Scarce had I put to sea,
  Bearing the maid with me, —
  Fairest of all was she
      Among the Norsemen ! —
  When on the white sea-strand,
  Waving his armèd hand,
  Saw we old Hildebrand,
      With twenty horsemen.

12

" Then launched they to the blast,
  Bent like a reed each mast,
  Yet we were gaining fast,
     When the wind failed us ;
  And with a sudden flaw
  Came round the gusty Skaw,
  So that our foe we saw
     Laugh as he hailed us.

" And as to catch the gale
  Round veered the flapping sail,
  Death ! was the helmsman's hail,
     Death without quarter !
  Mid-ships with iron keel
  Struck we her ribs of steel ;
  Down her black hulk did reel
     Through the black water !

" As with his wings aslant,
  Sails the fierce cormorant,
  Seeking some rocky haunt,
      With his prey laden,
  So toward the open main,
  Beating to sea again,
  Through the wild hurricane,
      Bore I the maiden.

" Three weeks we westward bore,
  And when the storm was o'er,
  Cloud-like we saw the shore
      Stretching to lee-ward ;
  There for my lady's bower
  Built I the lofty tower,
  Which, to this very hour,
      Stands looking sea-ward.

" There lived we many years ;
  Time dried the maiden's tears ;
  She had forgot her fears,
   She was a mother ;
  Death closed her mild blue eyes;
  Under that tower she lies ;
  Ne'er shall the sun arise
   On such another !

" Still grew my bosom then,
  Still as a stagnant fen !
  Hateful to me were men,
   The sun-light hateful !
  In the vast forest here,
  Clad in my warlike gear,
  Fell I upon my spear,
   O, death was grateful !

" Thus, seamed with many scars
Bursting these prison bars,
Up to its native stars
   My soul ascended !
There from the flowing bowl
Deep drinks the warrior's soul,
Skoal ! to the Northland ! *skoal !* " *
   — Thus the tale ended.

  * In Scandanavia this is the customary salutation when drinking a health. I have slightly changed the orthography of the word, in order to preserve the correct pronunciation.

THE WRECK OF THE HESPERUS.

—————

It was the schooner Hesperus,
   That sailed the wintry sea ;
And the skipper had taken his little daughtèr,
   To bear him company.

Blue were her eyes as the fairy-flax,
   Her cheeks like the dawn of day,
And her bosom white as the hawthorn buds,
   That ope in the month of May.

The skipper he stood beside the helm,
    His pipe was in his mouth,
And he watched how the veering flaw did blow
    The smoke now West, now South.

Then up and spake an old Sailòr,
    Had sailed the Spanish Main,
" I pray thee, put into yonder port,
    For I fear a hurricane.

" Last night, the moon had a golden ring,
    And to-night no moon we see ! "
The skipper, he blew a whiff from his pipe,
    And a scornful laugh laughed he.

Colder and louder blew the wind,
    A gale from the Northeast ;
The snow fell hissing in the brine,
    And the billows frothed like yeast.

Down came the storm, and smote amain,
    The vessel in its strength;
She shuddered and paused, like a frighted steed,
    Then leaped her cable's length.

"Come hither! come hither! my little daughter,
    And do not tremble so;
For I can weather the roughest gale,
    That ever wind did blow."

He wrapped her warm in his seaman's coat
    Against the stinging blast;
He cut a rope from a broken spar,
    And bound her to the mast.

"O father! I hear the church-bells ring,
    O say, what may it be?"
"'T is a fog-bell on a rock-bound coast!"—
    And he steered for the open sea.

" O father ! I hear the sound of guns,
    O say, what may it be ? "
" Some ship in distress, that cannot live
    In such an angry sea ! "

" O father ! I see a gleaming light,
    O say, what may it be ? "
But the father answered never a word,
    A frozen corpse was he.

Lashed to the helm, all stiff and stark,
    With his face turned to the skies,
The lantern gleamed through the gleaming snow
    On his fixed and glassy eyes.

Then the maiden clasped her hands and prayed
    That savèd she might be ;
And she thought of Christ, who stilled the wave,
    On the Lake of Galilee.

And fast through the midnight dark and drear,
    Through the whistling sleet and snow,
Like a sheeted ghost, the vessel swept
    Towards the reef of Norman's Woe.

And ever the fitful gusts between
    A sound came from the land ;
It was the sound of the trampling surf,
    On the rocks and the hard sea-sand.

The breakers were right beneath her bows,
    She drifted a dreary wreck,
And a whooping billow swept the crew
    Like icicles from her deck.

She struck where the white and fleecy waves
    Looked soft as carded wool,
But the cruel rocks, they gored her side
    Like the horns of an angry bull.

Her rattling shrouds, all sheathed in ice,
    With the masts went by the board ;
Like a vessel of glass, she stove and sank,
    Ho ! ho ! the breakers roared !

At daybreak, on the bleak sea-beach,
    A fisherman stood aghast,
To see the form of a maiden fair,
    Lashed close to a drifting mast.

The salt sea was frozen on her breast,
    The salt tears in her eyes ;
And he saw her hair, like the brown sea-weed,
    On the billows fall and rise.

Such was the wreck of the Hesperus,
    In the midnight and the snow !
Christ save us all from a death like this,
    On the reef of Norman's Woe !

THE LUCK OF EDENHALL.

FROM THE GERMAN OF UHLAND.

[The tradition, upon which this ballad is founded, and the " shards of the Luck of Edenhall," still exist in England. The goblet is in the possession of Sir Christopher Musgrave, Bart., of Eden Hall, Cumberland; and is not so entirely shattered, as the ballad leaves it.]

OF Edenhall, the youthful Lord
Bids sound the festal trumpet's call ;
He rises at the banquet board,
And cries, 'mid the drunken revellers all,
" Now bring me the Luck of Edenhall ! "

The butler hears the words with pain,
The house's oldest seneschal,
Takes slow from its silken cloth again
The drinking glass of crystal tall ;
They call it The Luck of Edenhall.

Then said the Lord ; " This glass to praise,
Fill with red wine from Portugal ! "
The gray-beard with trembling hand obeys ;
A purple light shines over all,
It beams from the Luck of Edenhall.

Then speaks the Lord, and waves it light,
" This glass of flashing crystal tall
Gave to my sires the Fountain-Sprite ;
She wrote in it ; *If this glass doth fall
Farewell then, O Luck of Edenhall !*

" 'T was right a goblet the Fate should be
    Of the joyous race of Edenhall !
    Deep draughts drink we right willingly ;
    And willingly ring, with merry call,
    Kling ! klang ! to the Luck of Edenhall ! "

First rings it deep, and full, and mild,
    Like to the song of a nightingale ;
    Then like the roar of a torrent wild ;
    Then mutters at last like the thunder's fall,
    The glorious Luck of Edenhall.

" For its keeper takes a race of might,
    The fragile goblet of crystal tall ;
    It has lasted longer than is right ;
    Kling ! klang ! — with a harder blow than all
    Will I try the Luck of Edenhall ! "

As the goblet ringing flies apart,
Suddenly cracks the vaulted hall;
And through the rift, the wild flames start;
The guests in dust are scattered all,
With the breaking Luck of Edenhall!

In storms the foe, with fire and sword;
He in the night had scaled the wall,
Slain by the sword lies the youthful Lord,
But holds in his hand the crystal tall,
The shattered Luck of Edenhall.

On the morrow the butler gropes alone,
The gray-beard in the desert hall,
He seeks his Lord's burnt skeleton,
He seeks in the dismal ruin's fall
The shards of the Luck of Edenhall.

" The stone wall," saith he, " doth fall aside,
 Down must the stately columns fall ;
 Glass is this earth's Luck and Pride ;
 In atoms shall fall this earthly ball
 One day like the Luck of Edenhall ! "

193

THE ELECTED KNIGHT.

FROM THE DANISH.

[The following strange and somewhat mystical ballad is
from Nyerup and Rahbek's *Danske Viser* of the Middle
Ages. It seems to refer to the first preaching of Christianity
in the North, and to the institution of Knight-Errantry.
The three maidens I suppose to be Faith, Hope, and Charity.
The irregularities of the original have been carefully pre-
served in the translation.]

———

Sɪʀ Oʟᴜꜰ he rideth over the plain,

  Full seven miles broad and seven miles wide,

But never, ah never can meet with the man

    A tilt with him dare ride.

      13

He saw under the hill-side
    A Knight full well equipped ;
His steed was black, his helm was barred ;
    He was riding at full speed.

He wore upon his spurs
    Twelve little golden birds ;
Anon he spurred his steed with a clang,
    And there sat all the birds and sang.

He wore upon his mail
    Twelve little golden wheels ,
Anon in eddies the wild wind blew,
    And round and round the wheels they flew.

He wore before his breast
    A lance that was poised in rest ;
And it was sharper than diamond-stone,
    It made Sir Oluf's heart to groan.

He wore upon his helm,
    A wreath of ruddy gold ;
And that gave him the Maidens Three,
    The youngest was fair to behold.

Sir Oluf questioned the Knight eftsoon
    If he were come from heaven down ;
" Art thou Christ of Heaven," quoth he,
    " So will I yield me unto thee."

" I am not Christ the Great,
    Thou shalt not yield thee yet ;
I am an Unknown Knight,
    Three modest Maidens have me bedight."

" Art thou a Knight elected,
    And have three Maidens thee bedight ;
So shalt thou ride a tilt this day,
    For all the Maidens' honor ! "

The first tilt they together rode
   They put their steeds to the test;
The second tilt they together rode,
   They proved their manhood best.

The third tilt they together rode,
   Neither of them would yield;
The fourth tilt they together rode,
   They both fell on the field.

Now lie the lords upon the plain,
   And their blood runs unto death;
Now sit the Maidens in the high tower,
   The youngest sorrows till death.

THE

CHILDREN

OF

THE LORD'S SUPPER.

FROM THE SWEDISH OF BISHOP TEGNÉR.

THE

CHILDREN OF THE LORD'S SUPPER.

———

PENTECOST, day of rejoicing, had come.   The
 church of the village
Gleaming stood in the morning's sheen.   On the
 spire of the belfry,
Tipped with a vane of metal, the friendly flames
 of the Spring-sun
Glanced like the tongues of fire, beheld by Apos-
 tles aforetime.

Clear was the heaven and blue, and May, with
    her cap crowned with roses,
Stood in her holiday dress in the fields, and the
    wind and the brooklet
Murmured gladness and peace, God's-peace!
    with lips rosy-tinted
Whispered the race of the flowers, and merry
    on balancing branches
Birds were singing their carol, a jubilant hymn to
    the Highest.
Swept and clean was the churchyard.   Adorned
    like a leaf-woven arbour
Stood its old-fashioned gate ; and within upon
    each cross of iron
Hung was a fragrant garland, new twined by the
    hands of affection.
Even the dial, that stood on a hillock among the
    departed,
(There full a hundred years had it stood,) was
    embellished with blossoms.

Like to the patriarch hoary, the sage of his kith
    and the hamlet,
Who on his birth-day is crowned by children and
    children's children,
So stood the ancient prophet, and mute with his
    pencil of iron
Marked on the tablet of stone, and measured the
    time and its changes,
While all around at his feet, an eternity slumber-
    ed in quiet.
Also the church within was adorned, for this was
    the season
When the young, their parents' hope, and the
    loved-ones of heaven,
Should at the foot of the altar renew the vows
    of their baptism.
Therefore each nook and corner was swept and
    cleaned, and the dust was
Blown from the walls and ceiling, and from the
    oil-painted benches.

There stood the church like a garden; the Feast
    of the Leafy Pavilions *
Saw we in living presentment. From noble arms
    on the church wall
Grew forth a cluster of leaves, and the preach-
    er's pulpit of oak-wood
Budded once more anew, as aforetime the rod
    before Aaron.
Wreathed thereon was the Bible with leaves, and
    the dove, washed with silver,
Under its canopy fastened, had on it a necklace of
    wind-flowers.
But in front of the choir, round the altar-piece
    painted by Hörberg,†
Crept a garland gigantic; and bright-curling tress-
    es of angels

---

  * The Feast of the Tabernacles; in Swedish, *Löfhyddo-högtiden*, the Leaf-huts'-high-tide.

  † The peasant-painter of Sweden. He is known chiefly by his altar-pieces in the village churches.

Peeped, like the sun from a cloud, from out of
the shadowy leaf-work.
Likewise the lustre of brass, new-polished, blinked
from the ceiling,
And for lights there were lilies of Pentecost set
in the sockets.

Loud rang the bells already; the thronging
crowd was assembled
Far from valleys and hills, to list to the holy
preaching.
Hark! then roll forth at once the mighty tones
from the organ,
Hover like voices from God, aloft like invisible
spirits.
Like as Elias in heaven, when he cast off from
him his mantle,
Even so cast off the soul its garments of earth;
and with one voice

Chimed in the congregation, and sang an anthem
    immortal
Of the sublime Wallin,* of David's harp in the
    North-land
Tuned to the choral of Luther ; the song on its
    powerful pinions
Took every living soul, and lifted it gently to
    heaven,
And every face did shine like the Holy One's
    face upon Tabor.
Lo ! there entered then into the church the Rev-
    erend Teacher.
Father he hight and he was in the parish ; a
    christianly plainness
Clothed from his head to his feet the old man of
    seventy winters.

---

* A distinguished pulpit-orator and poet. He is particu-
larly remarkable for the beauty and sublimity of his psalms.

Friendly was he to behold, and glad as the herald-
    ing angel

Walked he among the crowds, but still a contem-
    plative grandeur

Lay on his forehead as clear, as on moss-covered
    grave-stone a sun-beam.

As in his inspiration (an evening twilight that
    faintly

Gleams in the human soul, even now, from tne
    day of creation)

Th' Artist, the friend of heaven, imagines Saint
    John when in Patmos,

Gray, with his eyes uplifted to heaven, so seemed
    then the old man ;

Such was the glance of his eye, and such were
    his tresses of silver.

All the congregation arose in the pews that were
    numbered.

But with a cordial look, to the right and the left
    hand, the old man

Nodding all hail and peace, disappeared in the
    innermost chancel.

Simply and solemnly now proceeded the Chris-
    tian service,
Singing and prayer, and at last an ardent dis-
    course from the old man.
Many a moving word and warning, that out of
    the heart came
Fell like the dew of the morning, like manna on
    those in the desert.
Afterwards, when all was finished, the Teacher
    reëntered the chancel,
Followed therein by the young. On the right
    hand the boys had their places,
Delicate figures, with close-curling hair and
    cheeks rosy-blooming.
But on the left-hand of these, there stood the
    tremulous lilies,

Tinged with the blushing light of the morning,
    the diffident maidens, —
Folding their hands in prayer, and their eyes cast
    down on the pavement.
Now came, with question and answer, the cate-
    chism.   In the beginning
Answered the children with troubled and falter-
    ing voice, but the old man's
Glances of kindness encouraged them soon, and
    the doctrines eternal
Flowed, like the waters of fountains, so clear
    from lips unpolluted.
Whene'er the answer was closed, and as oft as
    they named the Redeemer,
Lowly louted the boys, and lowly the maidens all
    courtesied.
Friendly the Teacher stood, like an angel of light
    there among them,
And to the children explained he the holy, the
    highest, in few words,

Thorough, yet simple and clear, for sublimity
    always is simple,
Both in sermon and song, a child can seize on
    its meaning.
Even as the green-growing bud is unfolded when
    Spring-tide approaches
Leaf by leaf is developed, and, warmed by the
    radiant sunshine,
Blushes with purple and gold, till at last the per-
    fected blossom
Opens its odorous chalice, and rocks with its
    crown in the breezes,
So was unfolded here the Christian lore of sal-
    vation,
Line by line from the soul of childhood. The
    fathers and mothers
Stood behind them in tears, and were glad at
    each well-worded answer.

Now went the old man up to the altar ; — and
    straightway transfigured
(So did it seem unto me) was then the affection-
    ate Teacher.
Like the Lord's Prophet sublime, and awful as
    Death and as Judgment
Stood he, the God-commissioned, the soul-
    searcher, earthward descending.
Glances, sharp as a sword, into hearts, that to
    him were transparent
Shot he; his voice was deep, was low like the
    thunder afar off.
So on a sudden transfigured he stood there, he
    spake and he questioned.

"This is the faith of the Fathers, the faith the
    Apostles delivered,
This is moreover the faith whereunto I baptized
    you, while still ye

14

Lay on your mothers' breasts, and nearer the
    portals of heaven.
Slumbering received you then the Holy Church
    in its bosom ;
Wakened from sleep are ye now, and the light in
    its radiant splendor
Rains from the heaven downward ; — to-day on
    the threshold of childhood
Kindly she frees you again, to examine and make
    your election,
For she knows nought of compulsion, and only
    conviction desireth.
This is the hour of your trial, the turning-point
    of existence,
Seed for the coming days ; without revocation
    departeth
Now from your lips the confession ; Bethink ye,
    before ye make answer !
Think not, O think not with guile to deceive the
    questioning Teacher.

Sharp is his eye to-day, and a curse ever rests
    upon falsehood.

Enter not with a lie on Life's journey ; the mul-
    titude hears you,

Brothers and sisters and parents, what dear upon
    earth is and holy

Standeth before your sight as a witness ; the
    Judge everlasting

Looks from the sun down upon you, and angels
    in waiting beside him

Grave your confession in letters of fire, upon
    tablets eternal.

Thus then, — believe ye in God, in the Father
    who this world created ?

Him who redeemed it, the Son, and the Spirit
    where both are united ?

Will ye promise me here, (a holy promise !) to
    cherish

God more than all things earthly, and every man
    as a brother ?

Will ye promise me here, to confirm your faith
    by your living,
Th' heavenly faith of affection ! to hope, to for-
    give, and to suffer,
Be what it may your condition, and walk before
    God in uprightness ?
Will ye promise me this before God and man ? "
    — With a clear voice
Answered the young men Yes ! and Yes ! with
    lips softly-breathing
Answered the maidens eke. Then dissolved from
    the brow of the Teacher
Clouds with the thunders therein, and he spake
    in accents more gentle,
Soft as the evening's breath, as harps by Baby-
    lon's rivers.

  " Hail, then, hail to you all ! To the heir-
    dom of heaven be ye welcome !

Children no more from this day, but by covenant
    brothers and sisters !

Yet, — for what reason not children ? Of such
    is the kingdom of heaven.

Here upon earth an assemblage of children, in
    heaven one father,

Ruling them all as his household, — forgiving
    in turn and chastising,

That is of human life a picture, as Scripture has
    taught us.

Blessed are the pure before God ! Upon purity
    and upon virtue

Resteth the Christian Faith ; she herself from on
    high is descended.

Strong as a man and pure as a child, is the sum
    of the doctrine,

Which the Divine One taught, and suffered and
    died on the cross for.

O ! as ye wander this day from childhood's sa-
    cred asylum

Downward and ever downward, and deeper in
 Age's chill valley,
O ! how soon will ye come, — too soon ! — and
 long to turn backward
Up to its hill-tops again, to the sun-illumined,
 where Judgment
Stood like a father before you, and Pardon, clad
 like a mother,
Gave you her hand to kiss, and the loving heart
 was forgiven,
Life was a play and your hands grasped after the
 roses of heaven !
Seventy years have I lived already ; the father
 eternal
Gave me gladness and care ; but the loveliest
 hours of existence,
When I have steadfastly gazed in their eyes, I
 have instantly known them,
Known them all again ; — they were my child-
 hood's acquaintance.

Therefore take from henceforth, as guides in the
    paths of existence,
Prayer, with her eyes raised to heaven, and In-
    nocence, bride of man's childhood.
Innocence, child beloved, is a guest from the
    world of the blessed,
Beautiful, and in her hand a lily ; on life's roar-
    ing billows
Swings she in safety, she heedeth them not, in
    the ship she is sleeping.
Calmly she gazes around in the turmoil of men ;
    in the desert
Angels descend and minister unto her ; she her-
    self knoweth
Naught of her glorious attendance ; but follows
    faithful and humble,
Follows so long as she may her friend ; O do
    not reject her,
For she cometh from God and she holdeth the
    keys of the heavens. —

Prayer is Innocence' friend ; and willingly flyeth
    incessant

'Twixt the earth and the sky, the carrier-pigeon
    of heaven.

Son of Eternity, fettered in Time, and an exile,
    the Spirit

Tugs at his chains evermore, and struggles like
    flames ever upward.

Still he recalls with emotion his father's manifold
    mansions,

Thinks of the land of his fathers, where blos-
    somed more freshly the flowers,

Shone a more beautiful sun, and he played with
    the wingèd angels.

Then grows the earth too narrow, too close ; and
    homesick for heaven

Longs the wanderer again ; and the Spirit's long-
    ings are worship ;

Worship is called his most beautiful hour, and its
    tongue is entreaty.

Ah ! when the infinite burden of life descendeth
    upon us,
Crushes to earth our hope, and, under the earth,
    in tne grave-yard, —
Then it is good to pray unto God ; for his sor-
    rowing children
Turns he ne'er from his door, but he heals and
    helps and consoles them.
Yet is it better to pray when all things are pros-
    perous with us,
Pray in fortunate days, for life's most beautiful
    Fortune
Kneels down before the Eternal's throne ; and,
    with hands interfolded,
Praises thankful and moved the only giver of
    blessings.
Or do ye know, ye children, one blessing that
    comes not from Heaven ?
What has mankind forsooth, the poor ! that it has
    not received ?

Therefore, fall in the dust and pray !   The ser-
    aphs adoring

Cover with pinions six their face in the glory of
    him who

Hung his masonry pendant on naught, when the
    world he created.

Earth declareth his might, and the firmament ut-
    tereth his glory.

Races blossom and die, and stars fall downward
    from heaven,

Downward like withered leaves ; at the last
    stroke of midnight, millenniums

Lay themselves down at his feet, and he sees
    them, but counts them as nothing.

Who shall stand in his presence ?   The wrath
    of the judge is terrific,

Casting the insolent down at a glance.   When he
    speaks in his anger

Hillocks skip like the kid, and mountains leap
    like the roe-buck.

Yet, — why are ye afraid, ye children? This
    awful avenger,

Ah! is a merciful God! God's voice was not in
    the earthquake

Not in the fire, nor the storm, but it was in the
    whispering breezes.

Love is the root of creation; God's essence;
    worlds without number

Lie in his bosom like children; he made them
    for this purpose only.

Only to love and to be loved again, he breathed
    forth his spirit

Into the slumbering dust, and upright standing, it
    laid its

Hand on its heart, and felt it was warm with a
    flame out of heaven.

Quench, O quench not that flame! It is the
    breath of your being.

Love is life, but hatred is death. Not father, nor
    mother

Loved you, as God has loved you; for 't was
   . that you may be happy

Gave he his only son.   When he bowed down
   his head in the death-hour

Solemnized Love its triumph; the sacrifice then
   was completed.

Lo ! then was rent on a sudden the vail of the
   temple, dividing

Earth and heaven apart, and the dead from their
   sepulchres rising

Whispered with pallid lips and low in the ears of
   each other

Th' answer, but dreamed of before, to creation's
   enigma, —Atonement !

Depths of Love are Atonement's depths, for Love
   is Atonement.

Therefore, child of mortality, love thou the mer-
   ciful Father ;

Wish what the Holy One wishes, and not from
   fear, but affection ;

Fear is the virtue of slaves ; but the heart that
    loveth is willing ;
Perfect was before God, and perfect is Love,
    and Love only.
Lovest thou God as thou oughtest, then lovest
    thou likewise thy brethren ;
One is the sun in heaven, and one, only one, is
    Love also.
Bears not each human figure the godlike stamp on
    his forehead ?
Readest thou not in his face thine origin ? Is he
    not sailing
Lost like thyself on an ocean unknown, and is
    he not guided
By the same stars that guide thee ? Why shouldst
    thou hate then thy brother ?
Hateth he thee, forgive ! For 't is sweet to stam-
    mer one letter
Of the Eternal's language ; — on earth it is callèd
    Forgiveness !

Knowest thou Him, who forgave, with the crown
    of thorns round his temples ?

Earnestly prayed for his foes, for his murderers ?
    Say, dost thou know him ?

Ah ! thou confessest his name, so follow likewise
    his example,

Think of thy brother no ill, but throw a veil over
    his failings,

Guide the erring aright ; for the good, the heav-
    enly shepherd

Took the lost lamb in his arms, and bore it back
    to its mother.

This is the fruit of Love, and it is by its fruits that
    we know it.

Love is the creature's welfare, with God ; but
    Love among mortals

Is but an endless sigh !   He longs, and endures,
    and stands waiting,

Suffers and yet rejoices, and smiles with tears on
    his eyelids.

Hope, — so is called upon earth, his recompense,
    — Hope, the befriending,
Does what she can, for she points evermore up
    to heaven, and faithful
Plunges her anchor's peak in the depths of the
    grave, and beneath it
Paints a more beautiful world, a dim, but a sweet
    play of shadows !
Races, better than we, have leaned on her waver-
    ing promise,
Having naught else but Hope.   Then praise we
    our Father in heaven,
Him, who has given us more ; for to us has Hope
    been transfigured,
Groping no longer in night ; she is Faith, she is
    living assurance.
Faith is enlightened Hope ; she is light, is the eye
    of affection,
Dreams of the longing interprets, and carves
    their visions in marble.

Faith is the sun of life ; and her countenance
shines like the Hebrew's,

For she has looked upon God ; the heaven on
its stable foundation

Draws she with chains down to earth, and the
New Jerusalem sinketh

Splendid with portals twelve in golden vapors
descending.

There enraptured she wanders, and looks at the
figures majestic,

Fears not the wingèd crowd, in the midst of them
all is her homestead.

Therefore love and believe ; for works will follow
spontaneous

Even as day does the sun ; the Right from the
Good is an offspring,

Love in a bodily shape ; and Christian works are
no more than

Animate Love and faith, as flowers are the ani-
mate spring-tide.

Works do follow us all unto God; there stand
    and bear witness
Not what they seemed, — but what they were
    only. Blessed is he who
Hears their confession secure; they are mute
    upon earth until death's hand
Opens the mouth of the silent. Ye children,
    does Death e'er alarm you?
Death is the brother of Love, twin-brother is he,
    and is only
More austere to behold. With a kiss upon lips
    that are fading
Takes he the soul and departs, and rocked in
    the arms of affection,
Places the ransomed child, new born, 'fore the
    face of its father.
Sounds of his coming already I hear, — see dim-
    ly his pinions,
Swart as the night, but with stars strewn upon
    them! I fear not before him.
    15

Death is only release, and in mercy is mute.
    On his bosom
Freer breathes, in its coolness, my breast; and
    face to face standing
Look I on God as he is, a sun unpolluted by
    vapors;
Look on the light of the ages I loved, the spirits
    majestic,
Nobler, better than I; they stand by the throne
    all transfigured,
Vested in white, and with harps of gold, and are
    singing an anthem,
Writ in the climate of heaven, in the language
    spoken by angels.
You, in like manner, ye children beloved, he one
    day shall gather,
Never forgets he the weary;— then welcome, ye
    loved ones, hereafter!
Meanwhile forget not the keeping of vows, forget
    not the promise,

Wander from holiness onward to holiness; earth
    shall ye heed not;

Earth is but dust and heaven is light; I have
    pledged you to heaven.

God of the Universe, hear me! thou fountain of
    Love everlasting,

Hark to the voice of thy servant! I send up my
    prayer to thy heaven!

Let me hereafter not miss at thy throne one spirit
    of all these,

Whom thou hast given me here! I have loved
    them all like a father.

May they bear witness for me, that I taught them
    the way of salvation,

Faithful, so far as I knew of thy word; again
    may they know me,

Fall on their Teacher's breast, and before thy
    face may I place them,

Pure as they now are, but only more tried, and
    exclaiming with gladness,

Father, lo ! I am here, and the children, whom
    thou hast given me ! ''

Weeping he spake in these words ; and now at
    the beck of the old man
Knee against knee they knitted a wreath round
    the altar's enclosure.
Kneeling he read then the prayers of the conse-
    cration, and softly
With him the children read ; at the close, with
    tremulous accents,
Asked he the peace of heaven, a benediction
    upon them.
Now should have ended his task for the day ; the
    following Sunday
Was for the young appointed to eat of the Lord's
    holy Supper.
Sudden, as struck from the clouds, stood the
    Teacher silent and laid his

Hand on his forehead, and cast his looks upward;
　　while thoughts high and holy
Flew through the midst of his soul, and his eyes
　　glanced with wonderful brightness.
"On the next Sunday, who knows! perhaps I
　　shall rest in the grave-yard!
Some one perhaps of yourselves, a lily broken
　　untimely,
Bow down his head to the earth; why delay I?
　　the hour is accomplished.
Warm is the heart;—I will so! for to-day grows
　　the harvest of heaven.
What I began accomplish I now; for what fail-
　　ing therein is
I, the old man, will answer to God and the rev-
　　erend father.
Say to me only, ye children, ye denizens new-
　　come in heaven,
Are ye ready this day to eat of the bread of
　　Atonement?

What it denoteth, that know ye full well, I have
    told it you often.

Of the new covenant a symbol it is, of Atonement
    a token,

Stablished between earth and heaven. Man by
    his sins and transgressions

Far has wandered from God, from his essence.
    'T was in the beginning

Fast by the Tree of Knowledge he fell, and it
    hangs its crown o'er the

Fall to this day; in the Thought is the Fall; in
    the Heart the Atonement.

Infinite is the Fall, the Atonement infinite like-
    wise.

See ! behind me, as far as the old man remem-
    bers, and forward,

Far as Hope in her flight can reach with her
    wearied pinions,

Sin and Atonement incessant go through the life-
    time of mortals.

Brought forth is sin full-grown ; but Atonement
    sleeps in our bosoms
Still as the cradled babe ; and dreams of heaven
    and of angels,
Cannot awake to sensation ; is like the tones in
    the harp's strings,
Spirits imprisoned, that wait evermore the deliv-
    erer's finger.
Therefore, ye children beloved, descended the
    Prince of Atonement,
Woke the slumberer from sleep, and she stands
    now with eyes all resplendent,
Bright as the vault of the sky, and battles with
    Sin and o'ercomes her.
Downward to earth he came and transfigured,
    thence reascended,
Not from the heart in like wise, for there he still
    lives in the Spirit,
Loves and atones evermore. So long as Time
    is, is Atonement.

Therefore with reverence receive this day her
 visible token.

Tokens are dead if the things do not live.   The
 light everlasting

Unto the blind man is not, but is born of the eye
 that has vision.

Neither in bread nor in wine, but in the heart
 that is hallowed

Lieth forgiveness enshrined ; the intention alone
 of amendment

Fruits of the earth ennobles to heavenly things,
 and removes all

Sin and the guerdon of sin.   Only Love with
 his arms wide extended,

Penitence weeping and praying ; the Will that is
 tried, and whose gold flows

Purified forth from the flames ; in a word, man-
 kind by Atonement

Breaketh Atonement's bread, and drinketh Atone-
 ment's wine-cup.

But he who cometh up hither, unworthy, with
    hate in his bosom,

Scoffing at men and at God, is guilty of Christ's
    blessed body,

And the Redeemer's blood! To himself he
    eateth and drinketh

Death and doom! And from this, preserve us,
    thou heavenly Father!

Are ye ready, ye children, to eat of the bread
    of Atonement ? "

Thus with emotion he asked, and together an-
    swered the children

Yes! with deep sobs interrupted. Then read
    he the due supplications,

Read the Form of Communion, and in chimed
    the organ and anthem ;

O! Holy Lamb of God, who takest away our
    transgressions,

Hear us! give us thy peace! have mercy, have
    mercy upon us !

Th' old man, with trembling hand, and heavenly
    pearls on his eyelids,
Filled now the chalice and paten, and dealt round
    the mystical symbols.
O ! then seemed it to me, as if God, with the
    broad eye of mid-day,
Clearer looked in at the windows, and all the
    trees in the churchyard
Bowed down their summits of green, and the
    grass on the graves 'gan to shiver.
But in the children, (I noted it well ; I knew it)
    there ran a
Tremor of holy rapture along through their icy-
    cold members.
Decked like an altar before them, there stood
    the green earth, and above it
Heaven opened itself, as of old before Stephen ;
    they saw there
Radiant in glory the Father, and on his right
    hand the Redeemer.

Under them hear they the clang of harpstrings,
    and angels from gold clouds
Beckon to them like brothers, and fan with their
    pinions of purple.

Closed was the Teacher's task, and with heav-
    en in their hearts and their faces,
Up rose the children all, and each bowed him,
    weeping full sorely,
Downward to kiss that reverend hand, but all of
    them pressed he
Moved to his bosom, and laid, with a prayer,
    his hands full of blessings,
Now on the holy breast, and now on the inno-
    cent tresses.

MISCELLANEOUS.

THE VILLAGE BLACKSMITH.

UNDER a spreading chestnut tree
   The village smithy stands ;
The smith, a mighty man is he,
   With large and sinewy hands ;
And the muscles of his brawny arms
   Are strong as iron bands.

His hair is crisp, and black, and long,
  His face is like the tan ;
His brow is wet with honest sweat,
  He earns whate'er he can,
And looks the whole world in the face,
  For he owes not any man.

Week in, week out, from morn till night,
  You can hear his bellows blow ;
You can hear him swing his heavy sledge,
  With measured beat and slow,
Like a sexton ringing the village bell,
  When the evening sun is low.

And children coming home from school
  Look in at the open door ;
They love to see the flaming forge,
  And hear the bellows roar,
And catch the burning sparks that fly
  Like chaff from a threshing floor.

He goes on Sunday to the church,
    And sits among his boys ;
He hears the parson pray and preach,
    He hears his daughter's voice,
Singing in the village choir,
    And it makes his heart rejoice.

It sounds to him like her mother's voice,
    Singing in Paradise !
He needs must think of her once more,
    How in the grave she lies ;
And with his hard, rough hand he wipes
    A tear out of his eyes.

Toiling, — rejoicing, — sorrowing,
    Onward through life he goes ;
Each morning sees some task begin,
    Each evening sees it close ;
Something attempted, something done,
    Has earned a night's repose.

16

Thanks, thanks to thee, my worthy friend,
　For the lesson thou hast taught!
Thus at the flaming forge of life
　Our fortunes must be wrought;
Thus on its sounding anvil shaped
　Each burning deed and thought!

ENDYMION.

THE rising moon has hid the stars ;
Her level rays, like golden bars,
    Lie on the landscape green,
    With shadows brown between.

And silver white the river gleams,
As if Diana, in her dreams,
    Had dropt her silver bow
    Upon the meadows low.

On such a tranquil night as this,
She woke Endymion with a kiss,
        When, sleeping in the grove,
        He dreamed not of her love.

Like Dian's kiss, unasked, unsought,
Love gives itself, but is not bought;
        Nor voice, nor sound betrays
        Its deep, impassioned gaze.

It comes, — the beautiful, the free,
The crown of all humanity, —
        In silence and alone
        To seek the elected one.

It lifts the boughs, whose shadows deep,
Are Life's oblivion, the soul's sleep,
        And kisses the closed eyes
        Of him, who slumbering lies.

O, weary hearts! O, slumbering eyes!
O, drooping souls, whose destinies
    Are fraught with fear and pain,
    Ye shall be loved again!

No one is so accursed by fate,
No one so utterly desolate,
    But some heart, though unknown,
    Responds unto his own.

Responds, — as if with unseen wings,
An angel touched its quivering strings;
    And whispers, in its song,
    "Where hast thou stayed so long!"

THE TWO LOCKS OF HAIR.

FROM THE GERMAN OF PFIZER.

A YOUTH, light-hearted and content,
   I wander through the world ;
Here, Arab-like, is pitched my tent
   And straight again is furled.

Yet oft I dream, that once a wife
   Close in my heart was locked,
And in the sweet repose of life
   A blessed child I rocked.

I wake ! Away that dream, — away !
   Too long did it remain !
So long, that both by night and day
   It ever comes again.

The end lies ever in my thought ;
   To a grave so cold and deep
The mother beautiful was brought ;
   Then dropt the child asleep.

But now the dream is wholly o'er,
   I bathe mine eyes and see ;
And wander through the world once more,
   A youth so light and free.

Two locks, — and they are wondrous fair, —
   Left me that vision mild ;
The brown is from the mother's hair,
   The blond is from the child.

And when I see that lock of gold,
Pale grows the evening-red ;
And when the dark lock I behold,
I wish that I were dead.

IT IS NOT ALWAYS MAY.

NO HAY PÁJAROS EN LOS NIDOS DE ANTAÑO.
Spanish Proverb.

THE sun is bright, — the air is clear,
  The darting swallows soar and sing,
And from the stately elms I hear
  The blue-bird prophesying Spring.

So blue yon winding river flows,
  It seems an outlet from the sky,
Where waiting till the west wind blows,
  The freighted clouds at anchor lie.

All things are new ; — the buds, the leaves,
　　That gild the elm-tree's nodding crest,
And even the nest beneath the eaves ; —
　　There are no birds in last year's nest !

All things rejoice in youth and love,
　　The fulness of their first delight !
And learn from the soft heavens above
　　The melting tenderness of night.

Maiden, that read'st this simple rhyme,
　　Enjoy thy youth, it will not stay ;
Enjoy the fragrance of thy prime,
　　For O ! it is not always May !

Enjoy the Spring of Love and Youth,
　　To some good angel leave the rest ;
For Time will teach thee soon the truth,
　　There are no birds in last year's nest !

THE RAINY DAY.

THE day is cold, and dark, and dreary ;
It rains, and the wind is never weary ;
The vine still clings to the mouldering wall,
But at every gust the dead leaves fall,
    And the day is dark and dreary.

My life is cold, and dark, and dreary ;
It rains, and the wind is never weary ;
My thoughts still cling to the mouldering Past,
But the hopes of youth fall thick in the blast
    And the days are dark and dreary.

Be still, sad heart ! and cease repining ;
Behind the clouds is the sun still shining ;
Thy fate is the common fate of all,
Into each life some rain must fall,
    Some days must be dark and dreary.

GOD'S-ACRE.

I LIKE that ancient Saxon phrase, which calls
  The burial-ground God's-Acre! It is just;
It consecrates each grave within its walls,
  And breathes a benison o'er the sleeping dust.

God's-Acre! Yes, that blessed name imparts
  Comfort to those, who in the grave have sown
The seed, that they had garnered in their hearts,
  Their bread of life, alas! no more their own.

Into its furrows shall we all be cast,
 In the sure faith, that we shall rise again
At the great harvest, when the arch-angel's blast
 Shall winnow, like a fan, the chaff and grain.

Then shall the good stand in immortal bloom,
 In the fair gardens of that second birth;
And each bright blossom, mingle its perfume
 With that of flowers, which never bloomed on
  earth.

With thy rude ploughshare, Death, turn up the sod,
 And spread the furrow for the seed we sow;
This is the field and Acre of our God,
 This is the place, where human harvests grow!

TO THE RIVER CHARLES.

RIVER! that in silence windest
   Through the meadows, bright and free,
Till at length thy rest thou findest
   In the bosom of the sea!

Four long years of mingled feeling,
   Half in rest, and half in strife,
I have seen thy waters stealing
   Onward, like the stream of life.

Thou has taught me, Silent River !
　Many a lesson, deep and long ;
Thou hast been a generous giver ;
　I can give thee but a song.

Oft in sadness and in illness,
　I have watched thy current glide,
Till the beauty of its stillness
　Overflowed me, like a tide.

And in better hours and brighter,
　When I saw thy waters gleam,
I have felt my heart beat lighter,
　And leap onward with thy stream.

Not for this alone I love thee,
　Nor because, thy waves of blue
From celestial seas above thee
　Take their own celestial hue.

Where yon shadowy woodlands hide thee,
  And thy waters disappear,
Friends I love have dwelt beside thee,
  And have made thy margin dear.

More than this ; — thy name reminds me
  Of three friends, all true and tried ;
And that name, like magic, binds me
  Closer, closer to thy side.

Friends my soul with joy remembers !
  How like quivering flames they start,
When I fan the living embers
  On the hearth-stone of my heart !

'T is for this, thou Silent River !
  That my spirit leans to thee ;
Thou hast been a generous giver,
  Take this idle song from me.

17

BLIND BARTIMEUS.

Blind Bartimeus at the gates
Of Jericho in darkness waits;
He hears the crowd;— he hears a breath
Say, "It is Christ of Nazareth!"
And calls, in tones of agony,
Ἰησοῦ, ἐλέησόν με!

The thronging multitudes increase ;
Blind Bartimeus, hold thy peace !
But still, above the noisy crowd,
The beggar's cry is shrill and loud ;
Until they say, " He calleth thee ! "
Θάρσει, ἔγειραι, φωνεῖ σε !

Then saith the Christ, as silent stands
The crowd, " What wilt thou at my hands ? "
And he replies, " O give me light !
Rabbi, restore the blind man's sight ! "
And Jesus answers, *Ὕπαγε·*
Ἡ πίστις σου σέσωκέ σε !

Ye that have eyes, yet cannot see,
In darkness and in misery,
Recall those mighty Voices Three,
Ἰησοῦ, ἐλέησόν με !
Θάρσει, ἔγειραι, ὕπαγε !
Ἡ πίστις σου σέσωκέ σε !

THE GOBLET OF LIFE.

FILLED is Life's goblet to the brim;
And though my eyes with tears are dim,
I see its sparkling bubbles swim,
And chaunt a melancholy hymn
    With solemn voice and slow.

No purple flowers, — no garlands green,
Conceal the goblet's shade or sheen,
Nor maddening draughts of Hippocrene,
Like gleams of sunshine, flash between
    Thick leaves of misletoe.

This goblet, wrought with curious art,
Is filled with waters, that upstart,
When the deep fountains of the heart,
By strong convulsions rent apart,
    Are running all to waste.

And as it mantling passes round,
With fennel is it wreathed and crowned,
Whose seed and foliage sun-imbrowned
Are in its waters steeped and drowned,
    And give a bitter taste.

Above the lowly plants it towers,
The fennel, with its yellow flowers,
And in an earlier age than ours
Was gifted with the wondrous powers,
    Lost vision to restore.

It gave new strength, and fearless mood ;
And gladiators, fierce and rude,
Mingled it in their daily food ;
And he who battled and subdued,
  A wreath of fennel wore.

Then in Life's goblet freely press,
The leaves that give it bitterness,
Nor prize the colored waters less,
For in thy darkness and distress
  New light and strength they give !

And he who has not learned to know
How false its sparkling bubbles show,
How bitter are the drops of woe,
With which its brim may overflow,
  He has not learned to live.

The prayer of Ajax was for light ;
Through all that dark and desperate fight,
The blackness of that noonday night,
He asked but the return of sight,
    To see his foeman's face.

Let our unceasing, earnest prayer
Be, too, for light, — for strength to bear
Our portion of the weight of care,
That crushes into dumb despair
    One half the human race.

O suffering, sad humanity !
O ye afflicted ones, who lie
Steeped to the lips in misery,
Longing, and yet afraid to die,
    Patient, though sorely tried !

I pledge you in this cup of grief,
Where floats the fennel's bitter leaf!
The Battle of our Life is brief, .
The alarm, — the struggle, — the relief, —
Then sleep we side by side.

MAIDENHOOD.

———

MAIDEN ! with the meek, brown eyes,
In whose orbs a shadow lies
Like the dusk in evening skies !

Thou whose locks outshine the sun,
Golden tresses, wreathed in one,
As the braided streamlets run !

Standing, with reluctant feet,
Where the brook and river meet,
Womanhood and childhood fleet !

Gazing, with a timid glance,
On the brooklet's swift advance,
On the river's broad expanse!

Deep and still, that gliding stream
Beautiful to thee must seem,
As the river of a dream.

Then why pause with indecision,
When bright angels in thy vision
Beckon thee to fields Elysian?

Seest thou shadows sailing by,
As the dove, with startled eye,
Sees the falcon's shadow fly?

Hearest thou voices on the shore,
That our ears perceive no more,
Deafened by the cataract's roar?

O, thou child of many prayers!
Life hath quicksands, — Life hath snares!
Care and age come unawares!

Like the swell of some sweet tune,
Morning rises into noon,
May glides onward into June.

Childhood is the bough, where slumbered
Birds and blossoms many-numbered; —
Age, that bough with snows encumbered.

Gather, then, each flower that grows,
When the young heart overflows,
To embalm that tent of snows.

Bear a lily in thy hand;
Gates of brass cannot withstand
One touch of that magic wand.

Bear through sorrow, wrong, and ruth,
In thy heart the dew of youth,
On thy lips the smile of truth.

O, that dew, like balm, shall steal
Into wounds, that cannot heal,
Even as sleep our eyes doth seal ;

And that smile, like sunshine, dart
Into many a sunless heart,
For a smile of God thou art.

EXCELSIOR.

———

THE shades of night were falling fast,
As through an Alpine village passed
A youth, who bore, 'mid snow and ice,
A banner with the strange device
      Excelsior !

His brow was sad; his eye beneath,
Flashed like a faulchion from its sheath,
And like a silver clarion rung
The accents of that unknown tongue,
      Excelsior !

In happy homes he saw the light
Of household fires gleam warm and bright ;
Above, the spectral glaciers shone,
And from his lips escaped a groan,
    Excelsior !

" Try not the Pass ! " the old man said ;
" Dark lowers the tempest overhead,
The roaring torrent is deep and wide ! "
And loud that clarion voice replied
    Excelsior !

" O stay," the maiden said, " and rest
Thy weary head upon this breast ! "
A tear stood in his bright blue eye,
But still he answered, with a sigh,
    Excelsior !

" Beware the pine-tree's withered branch !
Beware the awful avalanche ! "
This was the peasant's last Good-night,
A voice replied, far up the height,
     Excelsior !

At break of day, as heavenward
The pious monks of Saint Bernard
Uttered the oft-repeated prayer,
A voice cried through the startled air
     Excelsior !

A traveller, by the faithful hound,
Half-buried in the snow was found,
Still grasping in his hand of ice
That banner with the strange device
     Excelsior !

There in the twilight cold and gray,
Lifeless, but beautiful, he lay,
And from the sky, serene and far,
A voice fell, like a falling star,
    Excelsior !

POEMS ON SLAVERY.

1842.

18

[The following poems, with one exception, were written at sea, in the latter part of October. I had not then heard of Dr. Channing's death. Since that event, the poem addressed to him is no longer appropriate. I have decided, however, to let it remain as it was written, a feeble testimony of my admiration for a great and good man.]

TO WILLIAM E. CHANNING.

THE pages of thy book I read,
    And as I closed each one,
My heart, responding, ever said,
    " Servant of God! well done!"

Well done! Thy words are great and bold;
    At times they seem to me,
Like Luther's, in the days of old,
    Half-battles for the free.

Go on, until this land revokes
  The old and chartered Lie,
The feudal curse, whose whips and yokes
  Insult humanity.

A voice is ever at thy side
  Speaking in tones of might,
Like the prophetic voice, that cried
  To John in Patmos, "Write!"

Write! and tell out this bloody tale;
  Record this dire eclipse,
This Day of Wrath, this Endless Wail,
  This dread Apocalypse!

THE SLAVE'S DREAM.

BESIDE the ungathered rice he lay,
　His sickle in his hand;
His breast was bare, his matted hair
　Was buried in the sand.
Again, in the mist and shadow of sleep,
　He saw his Native Land.

Wide through the landscape of his dreams
  The lordly Niger flowed;
Beneath the palm-trees on the plain
  Once more a king he strode;
And heard the tinkling caravans
  Descend the mountain-road.

He saw once more his dark-eyed queen
  Among her children stand;
They clasped his neck, they kissed his cheeks,
  They held him by the hand! —
A tear burst from the sleeper's lids
  And fell into the sand.

And then at furious speed he rode
  Along the Niger's bank;
His bridle-reins were golden chains,
  And, with a martial clank,
At each leap he could feel his scabbard of steel
  Smiting his stallion's flank.

Before him, like a blood-red flag,
   The bright flamingoes flew;
From morn till night he followed their flight,
   O'er plains where the tamarind grew,
Till he saw the roofs of Caffre huts,
   And the ocean rose to view.

At night he heard the lion roar,
   And the hyæna scream,
And the river-horse, as he crushed the reeds
   Beside some hidden stream;
And it passed, like a glorious roll of drums,
   Through the triumph of his dream.

The forests, with their myriad tongues,
   Shouted of liberty;
And the Blast of the Desert cried aloud,
   With a voice so wild and free,
That he started in his sleep and smiled
   At their tempestuous glee.

He did not feel the driver's whip,
   Nor the burning heat of day;
For Death had illumined the Land of Sleep,
   And his lifeless body lay
A worn-out fetter, that the soul
   Had broken and thrown away!

THE GOOD PART,

THAT SHALL NOT BE TAKEN AWAY.

———

She dwells by Great Kenhawa's side,
   In valleys green and cool;
And all her hope and all her pride
   Are in the village school.

Her soul, like the transparent air
   That robes the hills above,
Though not of earth, encircles there
   All things with arms of love.

And thus she walks among her girls
  With praise and mild rebukes;
Subduing e'en rude village churls
  By her angelic looks.

She reads to them at eventide
  Of One who came to save;
To cast the captive's chains aside,
  And liberate the slave.

And oft the blessed time foretells
  When all men shall be free;
And musical, as silver bells,
  Their falling chains shall be.

And following her beloved Lord,
  In decent poverty,
She makes her life one sweet record
  And deed of charity.

For she was rich, and gave up all
   To break the iron bands
Of those who waited in her hall,
   And labored in her lands.

Long since beyond the Southern Sea
   Their outbound sails have sped,
While she, in meek humility,
   Now earns her daily bread.

It is their prayers, which never cease,
   That clothe her with such grace;
Their blessing is the light of peace
   That shines upon her face.

THE SLAVE IN THE DISMAL SWAMP.

In dark fens of the Dismal Swamp
   The hunted Negro lay;
He saw the fire of the midnight camp,
And heard at times a horse's tramp
   And a bloodhound's distant bay.

Where will-o'-the-wisps and glowworms shine,
   In bulrush and in brake;
Where waving mosses shroud the pine,
And the cedar grows, and the poisonous vine
   Is spotted like the snake;

Where hardly a human foot could pass,
  Or a human heart would dare,
On the quaking turf of the green morass
He crouched in the rank and tangled grass,
  Like a wild beast in his lair.

A poor old slave, infirm and lame;
  Great scars deformed his face;
On his forehead he bore the brand of shame,
And the rags, that hid his mangled frame,
  Were the livery of disgrace.

All things above were bright and fair,
  All things were glad and free;
Lithe squirrels darted here and there,
And wild birds filled the echoing air
  With songs of Liberty!

On him alone was the doom of pain,
From the morning of his birth;
On him alone the curse of Cain
Fell, like a flail on the garnered grain,
And struck him to the earth!

THE SLAVE SINGING AT MIDNIGHT.

———

Loud he sang the psalm of David!
He, a Negro and enslaved,
Sang of Israel's victory,
Sang of Zion, bright and free.

In that hour, when night is calmest,
Sang he from the Hebrew Psalmist,
In a voice so sweet and clear
That I could not choose but hear,

Songs of triumph, and ascriptions,
Such as reached the swart Egyptians,
When upon the Red Sea coast
Perished Pharaoh and his host.

And the voice of his devotion
Filled my soul with strange emotion;
For its tones by turns were glad,
Sweetly solemn, wildly sad.

Paul and Silas, in their prison,
Sang of Christ, the Lord arisen,
And an earthquake's arm of might
Broke their dungeon-gates at night.

But, alas! what holy angel
Brings the Slave this glad evangel?
And what earthquake's arm of might
Breaks his dungeon-gates at night?

THE WITNESSES.

In Ocean's wide domains,
  Half buried in the sands,
Lie skeletons in chains,
  With shackled feet and hands.

Beyond the fall of dews,
  Deeper than plummet lies,
Float ships, with all their crews,
  No more to sink nor rise.

19

There the black Slave-ship swims,
   Freighted with human forms,
Whose fettered, fleshless limbs
   Are not the sport of storms.

These are the bones of Slaves ;
   They gleam from the abyss ;
They cry, from yawning waves,
   " We are the Witnesses ! "

Within Earth's wide domains
   Are markets for men's lives ;
Their necks are galled with chains,
   Their wrists are cramped with gyves.

Dead bodies, that the kite
   In deserts makes its prey ;
Murders, that with affright
   Scare schoolboys from their play !

All evil thoughts and deeds;
   Anger, and lust, and pride;
The foulest, rankest weeds,
   That choke Life's groaning tide!

These are the woes of Slaves;
   They glare from the abyss;
They cry, from unknown graves,
   " We are the Witnesses!"

THE QUADROON GIRL.

THE Slaver in the broad lagoon
  Lay moored with idle sail;
He waited for the rising moon,
  And for the evening gale.

Under the shore his boat was tied,
  And all her listless crew
Watched the gray alligator slide
  Into the still bayou.

Odors of orange-flowers, and spice,
    Reached them from time to time,
Like airs that breathe from Paradise
    Upon a world of crime.

The Planter, under his roof of thatch,
    Smoked thoughtfully and slow ;
The Slaver's thumb was on the latch,
    He seemed in haste to go.

He said, "My ship at anchor rides
    In yonder broad lagoon ;
I only wait the evening tides,
    And the rising of the moon."

Before them, with her face upraised,
    In timid attitude,
Like one half curious, half amazed,
    A Quadroon maiden stood.

Her eyes were large, and full of light,
    Her arms and neck were bare;
No garment she wore save a kirtle bright,
    And her own long, raven hair.

And on her lips there played a smile
    As holy, meek, and faint,
As lights in some cathedral aisle
    The features of a saint.

" The soil is barren, — the farm is old;"
    The thoughtful Planter said;
Then looked upon the Slaver's gold,
    And then upon the maid.

His heart within him was at strife
    With such accursed gains;
For he knew whose passions gave her life,
    Whose blood ran in her veins.

But the voice of nature was too weak;
    He took the glittering gold !
Then pale as death grew the maiden's cheek,
    Her hands as icy cold.

The Slaver led her from the door,
    He led her by the hand,
To be his slave and paramour
    In a strange and distant land !

THE WARNING.

Beware! The Israelite of old, who tore
   The lion in his path,—when, poor and blind,
He saw the blessed light of heaven no more,
   Shorn of his noble strength and forced to grind
In prison, and at last led forth to be
A pander to Philistine revelry,—

Upon the pillars of the temple laid
   His desperate hands, and in its overthrow
Destroyed himself, and with him those who made
   A cruel mockery of his sightless woe ;
The poor, blind Slave, the scoff and jest of all,
Expired, and thousands perished in the fall !

There is a poor, blind Samson in this land,
   Shorn of his strength, and bound in bonds of
      steel,
Who may, in some grim revel, raise his hand,
   And shake the pillars of this Commonweal,
Till the vast Temple of our liberties
A shapeless mass of wreck and rubbish lies.

THE SPANISH STUDENT.

1843.

DRAMATIS PERSONÆ.

Victorian,
Hypolito, } . . . . . . *Students of Alcalá.*

The Count of Lara,
Don Carlos, } . . *Gentlemen of Madrid.*

The Archbishop of Toledo.

A Cardinal.

Beltran Cruzado, ... *Count of the Gipsies.*

Bartolomé Roman, ... *A young Gipsy.*

The Padre Cura of Guadarrama.

Pedro Crespo, ... *Alcalde.*

Pancho, ... *Alguacil.*

Francisco, ... *Lara's Servant.*

Chispa, ... *Victorian's Servant.*

Baltasar, ... *Innkeeper.*

Preciosa, ... *A Gipsy girl.*

Angelica, ... *A poor girl.*

Martina, ... *The Padre Cura's niece.*

Dolores, ... *Preciosa's maid.*

Gipsies, Musicians, &c.

THE SPANISH STUDENT.

ACT I.

SCENE I. *The* COUNT OF LARA'S *chambers.* *Night.*
The COUNT *in his dressing-gown, smoking and con-*
versing with DON CARLOS.

LARA.

YOU were not at the play to-night, Don Carlos ;
How happened it ?

DON CARLOS.

       I had engagements elsewhere.
Pray who was there ?

LARA.

       Why, all the town and court.
The house was crowded ; and the busy fans

Among the gayly dressed and perfumed ladies
Fluttered like butterflies among the flowers.
There was the Countess of Medina Celi ;
The Goblin Lady with her Phantom Lover,
Her Lindo Don Diego ; Doña Sol,
And Doña Serafina, and her cousins.

DON CARLOS.

What was the play ?

LARA.

It was a dull affair ;
One of those comedies in which you see,
As Lope says, the history of the world
Brought down from Genesis to the Day of Judg-
ment.
There were three duels fought in the first act,
Three gentlemen receiving deadly wounds,
Laying their hands upon their hearts, and saying,
" O, I am dead ! " a lover in a closet,
An old hidalgo, and a gay Don Juan,
A Doña Inez with a black mantilla,

Followed at twilight by an unknown lover,
Who looks intently where he knows she is not !

DON CARLOS.

Of course, the Preciosa danced to-night ?

LARA.

And never better.   Every footstep fell
As lightly as a sunbeam on the water.
I think the girl extremely beautiful.

DON CARLOS.

Almost beyond the privilege of woman !
I saw her in the Prado yesterday.
Her step was royal, — queen-like, — and her face
As beautiful as a saint's in Paradise.

LARA.

May not a saint fall from her Paradise,
And be no more a saint ?

DON CARLOS.

        Why do you ask ?

LARA.

Because I have heard it said this angel fell,

And, though she is a virgin outwardly,

Within she is a sinner ; like those panels

Of doors and altar-pieces the old monks

Painted in convents, with the Virgin Mary

On the outside, and on the inside Venus !

DON CARLOS.

You do her wrong ; indeed, you do her wrong !

She is as virtuous as she is fair.

LARA.

How credulous you are ! Why look you, friend,

There 's not a virtuous woman in Madrid,

In this whole city ! And would you persuade me

That a mere dancing-girl, who shows herself,

Nightly, half-naked, on the stage, for money,

And with voluptuous motions fires the blood

Of inconsiderate youth, is to be held

A model for her virtue ?

DON CARLOS.

        You forget

She is a Gipsy girl.

LARA.

And therefore won

The easier.

DON CARLOS.

Nay, not to be won at all !

The only virtue that a Gipsy prizes

Is chastity.   That is her only virtue.

Dearer than life she holds it.   I remember

A Gipsy woman, a vile, shameless bawd,

Whose craft was to betray the young and fair ;

And yet this woman was above all bribes.

And when a noble lord, touched by her beauty,

The wild and wizard beauty of her race,

Offered her gold to be what she made others,

She turned upon him, with a look of scorn,

And smote him in the face !

LARA.

And does that prove

That Preciosa is above suspicion ?

DON CARLOS.

It proves a nobleman may be repulsed

20

When he thinks conquest easy.   I believe
That woman, in her deepest degradation,
Holds something sacred, something undefiled,
Some pledge and keepsake of her higher nature,
And, like the diamond in the dark, retains
Some quenchless gleam of the celestial light!

LARA.

Yet Preciosa would have taken the gold.

DON CARLOS (*rising*).

I do not think so.

LARA.

I am sure of it.
But why this haste ?   Stay yet a little longer,
And fight the battles of your Dulcinea.

DON CARLOS.

'T is late.   I must begone, for if I stay
You will not be persuaded.

LARA.

Yes ; persuade me.

DON CARLOS.

No one so deaf as he who will not hear !

LARA.

No one so blind as he who will not see!

DON CARLOS.

And so good night. I wish you pleasant dreams,
And greater faith in woman. [*Exit.*

LARA.

Greater faith!

I have the greatest faith; for I believe
Victorian is her lover. I believe
That I shall be to-morrow; and thereafter
Another, and another, and another,
Chasing each other through her zodiac,
As Taurus chases Aries.

(*Enter* FRANCISCO *with a casket.*)

Well, Francisco,

What speed with Preciosa?

FRANCISCO.

None, my lord.

She sends your jewels back, and bids me tell **you**
She is not to be purchased by your gold.

LARA.

Then I will try some other way to win her.
Pray, dost thou know Victorian ?

FRANCISCO.

Yes, my lord ;
I saw him at the jeweller's to-day.

LARA.

What was he doing there ?

FRANCISCO.

I saw him buy
A golden ring, that had a ruby in it.

LARA.

Was there another like it ?

FRANCISCO.

One so like it
I could not choose between them.

LARA.

It is well.
To-morrow morning bring that ring to me.
Do not forget. Now light me to my bed.

[*Exeunt.*

SCENE II.

A street in Madrid. Enter CHISPA, *followed by musicians, with a bagpipe, guitars, and other instruments.*

CHISPA.

Abernuncio Satanas! and a plague on all lovers who ramble about at night, drinking the elements, instead of sleeping quietly in their beds. Every dead man to his cemetery, say I; and every friar to his monastery. Now, here 's my master, Victorian, yesterday a cow-keeper, and to-day a gentleman; yesterday a student, and to-day a lover; and I must be up later than the nightingale, for as the abbot sings so must the sacristan respond. God grant he may soon be married, for then shall all this serenading cease. Ay, marry! marry! marry! Mother, what does marry mean? It means to spin, to bear children, and to weep, my daughter! And, of a truth, there is something more in matrimony than the wedding-ring. (*To the musicians.*)   And now, gentlemen, Pax vobiscum! as the ass said to the cabbages.   Pray, walk this way ; and don't hang down your heads.   It is no disgrace to have an old father and a ragged shirt.   Now, look you, you are gentlemen who lead the life of crickets ; you enjoy hunger by day and noise by night.   Yet, I beseech you, for this once be not loud, but pathetic ; for it is a serenade to a damsel in bed, and not to the Man in the Moon. Your object is not to arouse and terrify, but to soothe and bring lulling dreams.   Therefore, each shall not play upon his instrument as if it were the only one in the universe, but gently, and with a certain modesty, according with the others.   Pray, how may I call thy name, friend ?

FIRST MUSICIAN.

Gerónimo Gil, at your service.

CHISPA.

Every tub smells of the wine that is in it.
Pray, Gerónimo, is not Saturday an unpleasant
day with thee?

FIRST MUSICIAN.

Why so ?

CHISPA.

Because I have heard it said that Saturday is
an unpleasant day with those who have but one
shirt. Moreover, I have seen thee at the tavern,
and if thou canst run as fast as thou canst drink,
I should like to hunt hares with thee. What in-
strument is that ?

FIRST MUSICIAN.

An Aragonese bagpipe.

CHISPA.

Pray, art thou related to the bagpiper of Bu-
jalance, who asked a maravedí for playing, and
ten for leaving off ?

FIRST MUSICIAN.

No, your honor.

CHISPA.

I am glad of it.   What other instruments have we ?

SECOND AND THIRD MUSICIANS.

We play the bandurria.

CHISPA.

A pleasing instrument.   And thou ?

FOURTH MUSICIAN.

The fife.

CHISPA.

I like it ; it has a cheerful, soul-stirring sound, that soars up to my lady's window like the song of a swallow.   And you others ?

OTHER MUSICIANS.

We are the singers, please your honor.

CHISPA.

You are too many.   Do you think we are going to sing mass in the cathedral of Córdova ? Four men can make but little use of one shoe, and I see not how you can all sing in one song.

But follow me along the garden wall. That is
the way my master climbs to the lady's window.
It is by the Vicar's skirts that the devil climbs
into the belfry. Come, follow me, and make no
noise.   [*Exeunt.*

SCENE III.

PRECIOSA's *chamber.*   *She stands at the open window.*

PRECIOSA.

How slowly through the lilac-scented air
Descends the tranquil moon !   Like thistle-down
The vapory clouds float in the peaceful sky ;
And sweetly from yon hollow vaults of shade
The nightingales breathe out their souls in song.
And hark ! what songs of love, what soul-like
      sounds,
Answer them from below !

SERENADE.

Stars of the summer night!
   Far in yon azure deeps,
Hide, hide your golden light!
   She sleeps!
My lady sleeps!
   Sleeps!

Moon of the summer night!
   Far down yon western steeps,
Sink, sink in silver light!
   She sleeps!
My lady sleeps!
   Sleeps!

Wind of the summer night!
   Where yonder woodbine creeps,
Fold, fold thy pinions light!
   She sleeps!
My lady sleeps!
   Sleeps!

Dreams of the summer night!
   Tell her, her lover keeps
Watch! while in slumbers light
      She sleeps!
My lady sleeps!
      Sleeps!

(*Enter* VICTORIAN *by the balcony.*)

VICTORIAN.

Poor, little dove!   Thou tremblest like a leaf!

PRECIOSA.

I am so frightened!   'T is for thee I tremble!
I hate to have thee climb that wall by night!
Did no one see thee?

VICTORIAN.

             None, my love, but thou.

PRECIOSA.

'T is very dangerous; and when thou art gone
I chide myself for letting thee come here
Thus stealthily by night.   Where hast thou been?
Since yesterday I have no news from thee.

VICTORIAN.

Since yesterday I 've been in Alcalá.

Ere long the time will come, sweet Preciosa,

When that dull distance shall no more divide us

And I no more shall scale thy wall by night

To steal a kiss from thee, as I do now.

PRECIOSA.

An honest thief, to steal but what thou givest.

VICTORIAN.

And we shall sit together unmolested,

And words of true love pass from tongue to

tongue,

As singing birds from one bough to another.

PRECIOSA.

That were a life indeed to make time envious !

I knew that thou wouldst visit me to-night.

I saw thee at the play.

VICTORIAN.

Sweet child of air !

Never did I behold thee so attired

And garmented in beauty as to-night !
What hast thou done to make thee look so fair ?

PRECIOSA.

Am I not always fair ?

VICTORIAN.

Ay, and so fair
That I am jealous of all eyes that see thee,
And wish that they were blind.

PRECIOSA.

I heed them not ;
When thou art present, I see none but thee !

VICTORIAN.

There 's nothing fair nor beautiful, but takes
Something from thee, that makes it beautiful.

PRECIOSA.

And yet thou leavest me for those dusty books.

VICTORIAN.

Thou comest between me and those books too
often !
I see thy face in every thing I see !

The paintings in the chapel wear thy looks,
The canticles are changed to sarabands,
And with the learned doctors of the schools
I see thee dance cachuchas.

PRECIOSA.

In good sooth,
I dance with learned doctors of the schools
To-morrow morning.

VICTORIAN.

And with whom, I pray ?

PRECIOSA.

A grave and reverend Cardinal, and his Grace
The Archbishop of Toledo.

VICTORIAN.

What mad jest
Is this ?

PRECIOSA.

It is no jest ; indeed it is not.

VICTORIAN.

Prithee, explain thyself.

PRECIOSA.

Why, simply thus.

Thou knowest the Pope has sent here into Spain
To put a stop to dances on the stage.

VICTORIAN.

I have heard it whispered.

PRECIOSA.

Now the Cardinal,

Who for this purpose comes, would fain behold
With his own eyes these dances ; and the Arch-
bishop
Has sent for me ——

VICTORIAN.

That thou may'st dance before them !

Now viva la cachucha !   It will breathe
The fire of youth into these gray old men !
'T will be thy proudest conquest !

PRECIOSA.

Saving one.

And yet I fear these dances will be stopped,
And Preciosa be once more a beggar.

VICTORIAN.

The sweetest beggar that e'er asked for alms ;
With such beseeching eyes, that when I saw thee
I gave my heart away !

PRECIOSA.

Dost thou remember
When first we met ?

VICTORIAN.

It was at Córdova,
In the cathedral garden.   Thou wast sitting
Under the orange trees, beside a fountain.

PRECIOSA.

'T was Easter-Sunday.   The full-blossomed trees
Filled all the air with fragrance and with joy.
The priests were singing, and the organ sounded,
And then anon the great cathedral bell.
It was the elevation of the Host.
We both of us fell down upon our knees,
Under the orange boughs, and prayed together.
I never had been happy till that moment.

VICTORIAN.

Thou blessed angel!

PRECIOSA.

                    And when thou wast gone
I felt an aching here.   I did not speak
To any one that day.   But from that day
Bartolomé grew hateful unto me.

VICTORIAN.

Remember him no more.   Let not his shadow
Come between thee and me.   Sweet Preciosa!
I loved thee even then, though I was silent!

PRECIOSA.

I thought I ne'er should see thy face again.
Thy farewell had a sound of sorrow in it.

VICTORIAN.

That was the first sound in the song of love!
Scarce more than silence is, and yet a sound.
Hands of invisible spirits touch the strings
Of that mysterious instrument, the soul,
And play the prelude of our fate.   We hear
The voice prophetic, and are not alone.

21

PRECIOSA.

That is my faith.   Dost thou believe these warn-
    ings ?

VICTORIAN.

So far as this.   Our feelings and our thoughts
Tend ever on, and rest not in the Present.
As drops of rain fall into some dark well,
And from below comes a scarce audible sound,
So fall our thoughts into the dark Hereafter,
And their mysterious echo reaches us.

PRECIOSA.

I have felt it so, but found no words to say it!
I cannot reason ; I can only feel!
But thou hast language for all thoughts and feel-
    ings.
Thou art a scholar ; and sometimes I think
We cannot walk together in this world !
The distance that divides us is too great !
Henceforth thy pathway lies among the stars ;
I must not hold thee back.

VICTORIAN.

Thou little skeptic !

Dost thou still doubt ?   What I most prize in
     woman
Is her affections, not her intellect !
The intellect is finite ; but the affections
Are infinite, and cannot be exhausted.
Compare me with the great men of the earth ;
What am I ?   Why, a pigmy among giants !
But if thou lovest, — mark me ! I say lovest,
The greatest of thy sex excels thee not !
The world of the affections is thy world,
Not that of man's ambition.   In that stillness
Which most becomes a woman, calm and holy,
Thou sittest by the fireside of the heart,
Feeding its flame.   The element of fire
Is pure.   It cannot change nor hide its nature,
But burns as brightly in a Gipsy camp
As in a palace hall.   Art thou convinced ?

PRECIOSA.

Yes, that I love thee, as the good love heaven ,
But not that I am worthy of that heaven.
How shall I more deserve it ?

VICTORIAN.

Loving more.

PRECIOSA.

I cannot love thee more ; my heart is full.

VICTORIAN.

Then let it overflow, and I will drink it,
As in the summer-time the thirsty sands
Drink the swift waters of the Manzanares,
And still do thirst for more.

A WATCHMAN (*in the street*).

Ave Maria

Purissima !   'T is midnight and serene !

VICTORIAN.

Hear'st thou that cry ?

PRECIOSA.

It is a hateful sound,

To scare thee from me !

VICTORIAN.

As the hunter's horn
Doth scare the timid stag, or bark of hounds
The moor-fowl from his mate.

PRECIOSA.

Pray, do not go !

VICTORIAN.

I must away to Alcalá to-night.
Think of me when I am away.

PRECIOSA.

Fear not !
I have no thoughts that do not think of thee.

VICTORIAN (*giving her a ring*).

And to remind thee of my love, take this ;
A serpent, emblem of Eternity ;
A ruby, — say, a drop of my heart's blood.

PRECIOSA.

It is an ancient saying, that the ruby
Brings gladness to the wearer, and preserves
The heart pure, and, if laid beneath the pillow,

Drives away evil dreams.   But then, alas !
It was a serpent tempted Eve to sin.

VICTORIAN.

What convent of barefooted Carmelites
Taught thee so much theology ?

PRECIOSA (*laying her hand upon his mouth*).

Hush ! Hush !
Good night ! and may all holy angels guard thee!

VICTORIAN.

Good night ! good night !   Thou art my guardian
    angel !
I have no other saint than thou to pray to !

(*He descends by the balcony.*)

PRECIOSA.

Take care, and do not hurt thee.   Art thou safe ?

VICTORIAN (*from the garden*).

Safe as my love for thee !   But art thou safe ?
Others can climb a balcony by moonlight
As well as I.   Pray, shut thy window close ;
I am jealous of the perfumed air of night
That from this garden climbs to kiss thy lips.

PRECIOSA (*throwing down her handkerchief*).

Thou silly child! Take this to blind thine eyes.
It is my benison!

VICTORIAN.

And brings to me
Sweet fragrance from thy lips, as the soft wind
Wafts to the out-bound mariner the breath
Of the beloved land he leaves behind.

PRECIOSA.

Make not thy voyage long.

VICTORIAN.

To-morrow night
Shall see me safe returned. Thou art the star
To guide me to an anchorage. Good night!
My beauteous star! My star of love, good night!

PRECIOSA.

Good night!

WATCHMAN (*at a distance*).

Ave Maria Purissima!

SCENE IV.

An inn on the road to Alcalá. BALTASAR *asleep on a
bench. Enter* CHISPA.

CHISPA.

And here we are, half-way to Alcalá, between
cocks and midnight. Body o' me! what an inn
this is! The lights out, and the landlord asleep.
Holá! ancient Baltasar!

BALTASAR (*waking*).

Here I am.

CHISPA.

Yes, there you are, like a one-eyed Alcalde in
a town without inhabitants. Bring a light, and
let me have supper.

BALTASAR.

Where is your master?

CHISPA.

Do not trouble yourself about him. We have

stopped a moment to breathe our horses ; and, if he chooses to walk up and down in the open air, looking into the sky as one who hears it rain, that does not satisfy my hunger, you know.   But be quick, for I am in a hurry, and every man stretches his legs according to the length of his coverlet.   What have we here ?

BALTASAR (*setting a light on the table*).

Stewed rabbit.

CHISPA (*eating*).

Conscience of Portalegre !   Stewed kitten, you mean !

BALTASAR.

And a pitcher of Pedro Ximenes, with a roasted pear in it.

CHISPA (*drinking*).

Ancient Baltasar, amigo !   You know how to cry wine and sell vinegar.   I tell you this is nothing but Vino Tinto of La Mancha, with a tang of the swine-skin.

BALTASAR.

I swear to you by Saint Simon and Judas, it is all as I say.

CHISPA.

And I swear to you, by Saint Peter and Saint Paul, that it is no such thing. Moreover, your supper is like the hidalgo's dinner, very little meat, and a great deal of table-cloth.

BALTASAR.

Ha! ha! ha!

CHISPA.

And more noise than nuts.

BALTASAR.

Ha! ha! ha! You must have your joke, Master Chispa. But shall I not ask Don Victorian in, to take a draught of the Pedro Ximenes?

CHISPA.

No; you might as well say, " Don't-you-want-some ? " to a dead man.

BALTASAR.

Why does he go so often to Madrid?

CHISPA.

For the same reason that he eats no supper.
He is in love. Were you ever in love, Baltasar?

BALTASAR.

I was never out of it, good Chispa. It has
been the torment of my life.

CHISPA.

What! are you on fire, too, old hay-stack?
Why, we shall never be able to put you out.

VICTORIAN (*without*).

Chispa!

CHISPA.

Go to bed, Pero Grullo, for the cocks are
crowing.

VICTORIAN.

Ea! Chispa! Chispa!

CHISPA.

Ea! Señor. Come with me, ancient Balta-
sar, and bring water for the horses. I will pay
for the supper, to-morrow.   [*Exeunt*.

SCENE V.

VICTORIAN's *chambers at Alcalá*. HYPOLITO *asleep in an arm-chair. He awakes slowly.*

HYPOLITO.

I must have been asleep! ay, sound asleep!
And it was all a dream.   O sleep, sweet sleep!
Whatever form thou takest, thou art fair,
Holding unto our lips thy goblet filled
Out of Oblivion's well, a healing draught!
The candles have burned low; it must be late.
Where can Victorian be?   Like Fray Carrillo,
The only place in which one cannot find him
Is his own cell.   Here 's his guitar, that seldom
Feels the caresses of its master's hand.
Open thy silent lips, sweet instrument!
And make dull midnight merry with a song

(*He plays and sings.*)

Padre Francisco!

Padre Francisco!

What do you want of Padre Francisco?

Here is a pretty young maiden

Who wants to confess her sins!

Open the door and let her come in,

I will shrive her from every sin.

(*Enter* VICTORIAN.)

VICTORIAN.

Padre Hypolito!   Padre Hypolito!

HYPOLITO.

What do you want of Padre Hypolito?

VICTORIAN.

Come, shrive me straight; for, if love be a sin,

I am the greatest sinner that doth live.

I will confess the sweetest of all crimes,

A maiden wooed and won.

HYPOLITO.

The same old tale

Of the old woman in the chimney corner,

Who, while the pot boils, says, " Come here,
    my child ;
I 'll tell thee a story of my wedding-day."

              VICTORIAN.

Nay, listen, for my heart is full ; so full
That I must speak.

              HYPOLITO.

            Alas ! that heart of thine
Is like a scene in the old play ; the curtain
Rises to solemn music, and lo ! enter
The eleven thousand virgins of Cologne !

              VICTORIAN.

Nay, like the Sibyl's volumes, thou shouldst say ;
Those that remained, after the six were burned,
Being held more precious than the nine together.
But listen to my tale.   Dost thou remember
The Gipsy girl we saw at Córdova
Dance the Romalis in the market-place ?

              HYPOLITO.

Thou meanest Preciosa.

VICTORIAN.

Ay, the same.

Thou knowest how her image haunted me
Long after we returned to Alcalá.
She 's in Madrid.

HYPOLITO.

I know it.

VICTORIAN.

And I 'm in love.

HYPOLITO.

And therefore in Madrid when thou shouldst be
In Alcalá.

VICTORIAN.

O pardon me, my friend,
If I so long have kept this secret from thee ;
But silence is the charm that guards such treasures,
And, if a word be spoken ere the time,
They sink again, they were not meant for us.

HYPOLITO.

Alas ! alas ! I see thou art in love.

Love keeps the cold out better than a cloak.
It serves for food and raiment.   Give a Spaniard
His mass, his olla, and his Doña Luisa, —
Thou knowest the proverb.   But pray tell me,
          lover,
How speeds thy wooing ?   Is the maiden coy ?
Write her a song, beginning with an *Ave ;*
Sing as the monk sang to the Virgin Mary,

> *Ave! cujus calcem clare*
> *Nec centenni commendare*
> *Sciret Seraph studio!*

VICTORIAN.

Pray, do not jest!   This is no time for it !
I am in earnest !

HYPOLITO.

          Seriously enamored ?
What, ho !   The Primus of great Alcalá
Enamored of a Gipsy ?   Tell me frankly,
How meanest thou ?

VICTORIAN.

I mean it honestly.

HYPOLITO.

Surely thou wilt not marry her !

VICTORIAN.

Why not ?

HYPOLITO.

She was betrothed to one Bartolomé,
If I remember rightly, a young Gipsy
Who danced with her at Córdova.

VICTORIAN.

They quarrelled,

And so the matter ended.

HYPOLITO.

But in truth

Thou wilt not marry her.

VICTORIAN.

In truth I will.

The angels sang in heaven when she was born !
She is a precious jewel I have found

22

Among the filth and rubbish of the world.
I 'll stoop for it ; but when I wear it here,
Set on my forehead like the morning star,
The world may wonder, but it will not laugh.

HYPOLITO.

If thou wear'st nothing else upon thy forehead,
'T will be indeed a wonder.

VICTORIAN.

      Out upon thee,
With thy unseasonable jests !   Pray, tell me,
Is there no virtue in the world ?

HYPOLITO.

      Not much.
What, think'st thou, is she doing at this moment ;
Now, while we speak of her ?

VICTORIAN.

      She lies asleep,
And, from her parted lips, her gentle breath
Comes like the fragrance from the lips of flowers.
Her tender limbs are still, and, on her breast,

The cross she prayed to, e'er she fell asleep,
Rises and falls with the soft tide of dreams,
Like a light barge safe moored.

HYPOLITO.

        Which means, in prose,
She 's sleeping with her mouth a little open !

VICTORIAN.

O, would I had the old magician's glass
To see her as she lies in child-like sleep !

HYPOLITO.

And wouldst thou venture ?

VICTORIAN.

        Ay, indeed I would !

HYPOLITO.

Thou art courageous.   Hast thou e'er reflected
How much lies hidden in that one word, *now* ?

VICTORIAN.

Yes ; all the awful mystery of Life !
I oft have thought, my dear Hypolito,
That could we, by some spell of magic, change

The world and its inhabitants to stone,

In the same attitudes they now are in,

What fearful glances downward might we cast

Into the hollow chasms of human life !

What groups should we behold about the death-
bed,

Putting to shame the group of Niobe !

What joyful welcomes, and what sad farewells !

What stony tears in those congealed eyes !

What visible joy or anguish in those cheeks !

What bridal pomps, and what funereal shows !

What foes, like gladiators, fierce and struggling !

What lovers with their marble lips together !

HYPOLITO.

Ay, there it is ! and, if I were in love,

That is the very point I most should dread.

This magic glass, these magic spells of thine,

Might tell a tale were better left untold.

For instance, they might show us thy fair cousin,

The Lady Violante, bathed in tears

Of love and anger, like the maid of Colchis,

Whom thou, another faithless Argonaut,

Having won that golden fleece, a woman's love,

Desertest for this Glaucè.

VICTORIAN.

            Hold thy peace !

She cares not for me.   She may wed another,

Or go into a convent, and, thus dying,

Marry Achilles in the Elysian Fields.

HYPOLITO (*rising*).

And so, good night ! Good morning, I should say.

       (*Clock strikes three.*)

Hark ! how the loud and ponderous mace of Time

Knocks at the golden portals of the day !

And so, once more, good night ! We 'll speak more largely

Of Preciosa when we meet again.

Get thee to bed, and the magician, Sleep,

Shall show her to thee, in his magic glass,

In all her loveliness.   Good night !   [*Exit.*

VICTORIAN.

Good night !

But not to bed ; for I must read awhile.

(*Throws himself into the arm-chair which* Hypolito *has left, and lays a large book open upon his knees.*)

Must read, or sit in reverie and watch
The changing color of the waves that break
Upon the idle seashore of the mind !
Visions of Fame ! that once did visit me,
Making night glorious with your smile, where are
    ye ?
O, who shall give me, now that ye are gone,
Juices of those immortal plants that bloom
Upon Olympus, making us immortal ?
Or teach me where that wondrous mandrake grows
Whose magic root, torn from the earth with groans,
At midnight hour, can scare the fiends away,
And make the mind prolific in its fancies ?
I have the wish, but want the will, to act !
Souls of great men departed !   Ye whose words

Have come to light from the swift river of Time,
Like Roman swords found in the Tagus' bed,
Where is the strength to wield the arms ye bore?
From the barred visor of Antiquity
Reflected shines the eternal light of Truth,
As from a mirror!   All the means of action —
The shapeless masses — the materials —
Lie everywhere about us.   What we need
Is the celestial fire to change the flint
Into transparent crystal, bright and clear.
That fire is genius!   The rude peasant sits
At evening in his smoky cot, and draws
With charcoal uncouth figures on the wall.
The son of genius comes, foot-sore with travel,
And begs a shelter from the inclement night.
He takes the charcoal from the peasant's hand,
And, by the magic of his touch at once
Transfigured, all its hidden virtues shine,
And, in the eyes of the astonished clown,
It gleams a diamond!   Even thus transformed,

Rude popular traditions and old tales

Shine as immortal poems, at the touch

Of some poor, houseless, homeless, wandering
        bard,

Who had but a night's lodging for his pains.

But there are brighter dreams than those of Fame,

Which are the dreams of Love ! Out of the heart

Rises the bright ideal of these dreams,

As from some woodland fount a spirit rises

And sinks again into its silent deeps,

Ere the enamored knight can touch her robe !

'T is this ideal that the soul of man,

Like the enamored knight beside the fountain,

Waits for upon the margin of Life's stream ;

Waits to behold her rise from the dark waters,

Clad in a mortal shape ! Alas ! how many

Must wait in vain ! The stream flows evermore,

But from its silent deeps no spirit rises !

Yet I, born under a propitious star,

Have found the bright ideal of my dreams.

Yes! she is ever with me.	I can feel,
Here, as I sit at midnight and alone,
Her gentle breathing! on my breast can feel
The pressure of her head!	God's benison
Rest ever on it!	Close those beauteous eyes,
Sweet Sleep! and all the flowers that bloom at
    night
With balmy lips breathe in her ears my name!

       (*Gradually sinks asleep.*)

ACT II.

SCENE I.   PRECIOSA's *chamber. Morning.*   PRECIOSA
and ANGELICA.

PRECIOSA.

WHY will you go so soon ?   Stay yet awhile.
The poor too often turn away unheard
From hearts that shut against them with a sound
That will be heard in heaven.   Pray, tell me more
Of your adversities.   Keep nothing from me.
What is your landlord's name ?

ANGELICA.

                    The Count of Lara.

PRECIOSA.

The Count of Lara ?   O, beware that man !
Mistrust his pity, — hold no parley with him !
And rather die an outcast in the streets
Than touch his gold.

ANGELICA.

You know him, then !

PRECIOSA.

As much

As any woman may, and yet be pure.
As you would keep your name without a blemish,
Beware of him !

ANGELICA.

Alas ! what can I do ?

I cannot choose my friends. Each word of kind-
   ness,
Come whence it may, is welcome to the poor.

PRECIOSA.

Make me your friend.   A girl so young and fair
Should have no friends but those of her own sex.
What is your name ?

ANGELICA.

Angelica.

PRECIOSA.

That name

Was given you, that you might be an angel

To her who bore you!   When your infant smile
Made her home Paradise, you were her angel.
O, be an angel still!   She needs that smile.
So long as you are innocent, fear nothing.
No one can harm you!   I am a poor girl,
Whom chance has taken from the public streets.
I have no other shield than mine own virtue.
That is the charm which has protected me!
Amid a thousand perils, I have worn it
Here on my heart!   It is my guardian angel.

ANGELICA (*rising*).

I thank you for this counsel, dearest lady.

PRECIOSA.

Thank me by following it.

ANGELICA.

Indeed I will.

PRECIOSA.

Pray, do not go.   I have much more to say.

ANGELICA.

My mother is alone.   I dare not leave her.

PRECIOSA.

Some other time, then, when we meet again.

You must not go away with words alone.

(*Gives her a purse.*)

Take this.   Would it were more.

ANGELICA.

I thank you, lady.

PRECIOSA.

No thanks.   To-morrow come to me again.

I dance to-night, — perhaps for the last time.

But what I gain, I promise shall be yours,

If that can save you from the Count of Lara.

ANGELICA.

O, my dear lady! how shall I be grateful

For so much kindness ?

PRECIOSA.

I deserve no thanks.

Thank Heaven, not me.

ANGELICA.

Both Heaven and you.

PRECIOSA.

Farewell

Remember that you come again to-morrow.

ANGELICA.

I will.   And may the blessed Virgin guard you,
And all good angels.   [*Exit*

PRECIOSA.

May they guard thee too,
And all the poor ; for they have need of angels.
Now bring me, dear Dolores, my basquiña,
My richest maja dress, — my dancing dress,
And my most precious jewels !   Make me look
Fairer than night e'er saw me !   I 've a prize
To win this day, worthy of Preciosa !

(*Enter* BELTRAN CRUZADO.)

CRUZADO.

Ave Maria !

PRECIOSA.

O God !   my evil genius !
What seekest thou here to-day ?

CRUZADO.

Thyself, — my child.

PRECIOSA.

What is thy will with me ?

CRUZADO.

Gold ! gold !

PRECIOSA.

I gave thee yesterday ; I have no more.

CRUZADO.

The gold of the Busné, — give me his gold !

PRECIOSA.

I gave the last in charity to-day.

CRUZADO.

That is a foolish lie.

PRECIOSA.

It is the truth.

CRUZADO.

Curses upon thee ! Thou art not my child !
Hast thou given gold away, and not to me ?
Not to thy father ? To whom, then ?

PRECIOSA.

To one
Who needs it more.

CRUZADO.

No one can need it more.

PRECIOSA.

Thou art not poor.

CRUZADO.

What, I, who lurk about
In dismal suburbs and unwholesome lanes ;
I, who am housed worse than the galley slave ,
I, who am fed worse than the kennelled hound ,
I, who am clothed in rags, — Beltran Cruzado, —
Not poor !

PRECIOSA.

Thou hast a stout heart and strong hands.
Thou canst supply thy wants ; what wouldst thou
more ?

CRUZADO.

The gold of the Busné ! give me his gold !

PRECIOSA.

Beltran Cruzado ! hear me once for all.
I speak the truth.   So long as I had gold,
I gave it to thee freely, at all times,
Never denied thee ; never had a wish
But to fulfil thine own.   Now go in peace !
Be merciful, be patient, and, ere long,
Thou shalt have more.

CRUZADO.

                    And if I have it not,
Thou shalt no longer dwell here in rich chambers,
Wear silken dresses, feed on dainty food,
And live in idleness ; but go with me,
Dance the Romalis in the public streets,
And wander wild again o'er field and fell ;
For here we stay not long.

PRECIOSA.

                    What ! march again ?

CRUZADO.

Ay, with all speed.   I hate the crowded town !

23

I cannot breathe shut up within its gates!
Air, — I want air, and sunshine, and blue sky,
The feeling of the breeze upon my face,
The feeling of the turf beneath my feet,
And no walls but the far-off mountain tops.
Then I am free and strong, — once more myself,
Beltran Cruzado, Count of the Calés!

PRECIOSA.

God speed thee on thy march! — I cannot go

CRUZADO.

Remember who I am, and who thou art!
Be silent and obey! Yet one thing more.
Bartolomé Román ——

PRECIOSA (*with emotion*).

O, I beseech thee!
If my obedience and blameless life,
If my humility and meek submission
In all things hitherto, can move in thee
One feeling of compassion; if thou art
Indeed my father, and canst trace in me
One look of her who bore me, or one tone

That doth remind thee of her, let it plead
In my behalf, who am a feeble girl,
Too feeble to resist, and do not force me
To wed that man !   I am afraid of him !
I do not love him !   On my knees I beg thee
To use no violence, nor do in haste
What cannot be undone !

CRUZADO.

　　　　　　　　　O child, child, child !
Thou hast betrayed thy secret, as a bird
Betrays her nest, by striving to conceal it.
I will not leave thee here in the great city
To be a grandee's mistress.   Make thee ready
To go with us ; and until then remember
A watchful eye is on thee.　　　　　　　[*Exit.*

PRECIOSA.

　　　　　　　　　Woe is me !
I have a strange misgiving in my heart !
But that one deed of charity I 'll do,
Befall what may ; they cannot take that from me.
　　　　　　　　　　　　　　　　[*Exit.*

SCENE II.

A room in the ARCHBISHOP's *Palace. The* ARCHBISHOP *and a* CARDINAL *seated.*

ARCHBISHOP.

Knowing how near it touched the public morals,
And that our age is grown corrupt and rotten
By such excesses, we have sent to Rome,
Beseeching that his Holiness would aid
In curing the gross surfeit of the time,
By seasonable stop put here in Spain
To bull-fights and lewd dances on the stage.
All this you know.

CARDINAL.

Know and approve.

ARCHBISHOP.

And farther,
That, by a mandate from his Holiness,
The first have been suppressed.

CARDINAL.

          I trust for ever,

It was a cruel sport.

ARCHBISHOP.

          A barbarous pastime,

Disgraceful to the land that calls itself
Most Catholic and Christian.

CARDINAL.

          Yet the people

Murmur at this ; and, if the public dances
Should be condemned upon too slight occasion,
Worse ills might follow than the ills we cure.
As *Panem et Circenses* was the cry,
Among the Roman populace of old,
So *Pan y Toros* is the cry in Spain.
Hence I would act advisedly herein ;
And therefore have induced your grace to see
These national dances, ere we interdict them.

        (Enter a Servant.)

SERVANT.

The dancing-girl, and with her the musicians
Your grace was pleased to order, wait without.

ARCHBISHOP.

Bid them come in.   Now shall your eyes behold
In what angelic yet voluptuous shape
The Devil came to tempt Saint Anthony.

(*Enter* PRECIOSA, *with a mantle thrown over her head.*
She advances slowly, in a modest, half-timid attitude.)

CARDINAL (*aside*).

O, what a fair and ministering angel
Was lost to heaven when this sweet woman fell !

PRECIOSA (*kneeling before the* ARCHBISHOP).

I have obeyed the order of your grace.
If I intrude upon your better hours,
I proffer this excuse, and here beseech
Your holy benediction.

ARCHBISHOP.

May God bless thee,
And lead thee to a better life.   Arise.

CARDINAL (*aside*).

Her acts are modest, and her words discreet!
I did not look for this!   Come hither, child.
Is thy name Preciosa.

PRECIOSA.

Thus I am called.

CARDINAL.

That is a Gipsy name.   Who is thy father?

PRECIOSA.

Beltran Cruzado, Count of the Calés.

ARCHBISHOP.

I have a dim remembrance of that man;
He was a bold and reckless character,
A sun-burnt Ishmael!

CARDINAL.

Dost thou remember
Thy earlier days?

PRECIOSA.

Yes; by the Darro's side
My childhood passed.   I can remember still

The river, and the mountains capped with snow,
The villages, where, yet a little child,
I told the traveller's fortune in the street;
The smuggler's horse, the brigand and the shep-
     herd;
The march across the moor; the halt at noon;
The red fire of the evening camp, that lighted
The forest where we slept; and, farther back,
As in a dream or in some former life,
Gardens and palace walls.

ARCHBISHOP.

                    'T is the Alhambra,
Under whose towers the Gipsy camp was pitched.
But the time wears; and we would see thee dance.

PRECIOSA.

Your grace shall be obeyed.

*(She lays aside her mantilla. The music of the cachucha
is played, and the dance begins. The* ARCHBISHOP *and
the* CARDINAL *look on with gravity and an occasional
frown; then make signs to each other; and, as the dance*

*continues, become more and more pleased and excited;
and at length rise from their seats, throw their caps in
the air, and applaud vehemently as the scene closes.)*

SCENE III.

*The Prado. A long avenue of trees leading to the gate of
Atocha. On the right the dome and spires of a convent.
A fountain. Evening.* DON CARLOS *and* HYPOLITO
meeting.

DON CARLOS.

Holá! good evening, Don Hypolito.

HYPOLITO.

And a good evening to my friend, Don Carlos.
Some lucky star has led my steps this way.
I was in search of you.

DON CARLOS.

   Command me always.

HYPOLITO.

Do you remember, in Quevedo's Dreams,

The miser, who, upon the Day of Judgment,
Asks if his money-bags would rise?

DON CARLOS.

                                        I do ;
But what of that ?

HYPOLITO.

            I am that wretched man.

DON CARLOS.

You mean to tell me yours have risen empty ?

HYPOLITO.

And amen ! said my Cid Campeador.

DON CARLOS.

Pray, how much need you ?

HYPOLITO.

                    Some half dozen ounces.
Which, with due interest ——

        DON CARLOS (*giving his purse*).

                        What, am I a Jew
To put my moneys out at usury ?
Here is my purse.

HYPOLITO.

Thank you.   A pretty purse,
Made by the hand of some fair Madrileña ;
Perhaps a keepsake.

DON CARLOS.

No, 't is at your service.

HYPOLITO.

Thank you again. Lie there, good Chrysos-
    tom,
And with thy golden mouth remind me often,
I am the debtor of my friend.

DON CARLOS.

But tell me,
Come you to-day from Alcalá ?

HYPOLITO.

This moment.

DON CARLOS.

And pray, how fares the brave Victorian ?

HYPOLITO.

Indifferent well ; that is to say, not well.

A damsel has ensnared him with the glances
Of her dark, roving eyes, as herdsmen catch
A steer of Andalusia with a lazo.
He is in love.

DON CARLOS.

And is it faring ill

To be in love ?

HYPOLITO.

In his case very ill.

DON CARLOS.

Why so ?

HYPOLITO.

For many reasons.   First and foremost,
Because he is in love with an ideal ;
A creature of his own imagination ;
A child of air ; an echo of his heart ;
And, like a lily on a river floating,
She floats upon the river of his thoughts !

DON CARLOS.

A common thing with poets.   But who is

This floating lily ?   For, in fine, some woman,
Some living woman, — not a mere ideal, —
Must wear the outward semblance of his thought.
Who is it ?   Tell me.

HYPOLITO.

Well, it is a woman !
But, look you, from the coffer of his heart
He brings forth precious jewels to adorn her,
As pious priests adorn some favorite saint
With gems and gold, until at length she gleams
One blaze of glory.   Without these, you know,
And the priest's benediction, 't is a doll.

DON CARLOS.

Well, well ! who is this doll ?

HYPOLITO.

Why, who do you think ?

DON CARLOS.

His cousin Violante.

HYPOLITO.

Guess again.

To ease his laboring heart, in the last storm
He threw her overboard, with all her ingots.

DON CARLOS.

I cannot guess ; so tell me who it is.

HYPOLITO.

Not I.

DON CARLOS.

Why not ?

HYPOLITO (*mysteriously*.)

Why ? Because Mari Franca
Was married four leagues out of Salamanca !

DON CARLOS.

Jesting aside, who is it ?

HYPOLITO.

Preciosa.

DON CARLOS.

Impossible !   The Count of Lara tells me
She is not virtuous.

HYPOLITO.

Did I say she was ?

The Roman Emperor Claudius had a wife
Whose name was Messalina, as I think ;
Valeria Messalina was her name.
But hist ! I see him yonder through the trees,
Walking as in a dream.

DON CARLOS.

He comes this way.

HYPOLITO.

It has been truly said by some wise man,
That money, grief, and love cannot be hidden.

(*Enter* VICTORIAN *in front.*)

VICTORIAN.

Where'er thy step has passed is holy ground !
These groves are sacred ! I behold thee walking
Under these shadowy trees, where we have walked
At evening, and I feel thy presence now ;
Feel that the place has taken a charm from thee,
And is for ever hallowed.

HYPOLITO.

Mark him well !

See how he strides away with lordly air,
Like that odd guest of stone, that grim Commander
Who comes to sup with Juan in the play.

DON CARLOS.

What ho ! Victorian !

HYPOLITO.

Wilt thou sup with us ?

VICTORIAN.

Holá! amigos !   Faith, I did not see you.
How fares Don Carlos ?

DON CARLOS.

At your service ever.

VICTORIAN.

How is that young and green-eyed Gaditana
That you both wot of ?

DON CARLOS.

Ay, soft, emerald eyes !
She has gone back to Cadiz.

HYPOLITO.

Ay de mí !

VICTORIAN.

You are much to blame for letting her go back.
A pretty girl ; and in her tender eyes
Just that soft shade of green we sometimes see
In evening skies.

HYPOLITO.

But, speaking of green eyes,
Are thine green ?

VICTORIAN.

Not a whit. Why so ?

HYPOLITO.

I think
The slightest shade of green would be becoming,
For thou art jealous.

VICTORIAN.

No, I am not jealous.

HYPOLITO.

Thou snouldst be.

VICTORIAN.

Why ?

24

HYPOLITO.

Because thou art in love.
And they who are in love are always jealous.
Therefore thou shouldst be.

VICTORIAN.

Marry, is that all ?
Farewell ; I am in haste.   Farewell, Don Carlos.
Thou sayest I should be jealous ?

HYPOLITO.

Ay, in truth
I fear there is reason.   Be upon thy guard.
I hear it whispered that the Count of Lara
Lays siege to the same citadel.

VICTORIAN.

Indeed !
Then he will have his labor for his pains.

HYPOLITO.

He does not think so, and Don Carlos tells me
He boasts of his success.

VICTORIAN.

How 's this, Don Carlos ?

DON CARLOS.

Some hints of it I heard from his own lips.
He spoke but lightly of the lady's virtue,
As a gay man might speak.

VICTORIAN.

Death and damnation!
I 'll cut his lying tongue out of his mouth,
And throw it to my dog! But no, no, no!
This cannot be. You jest, indeed you jest.
Trifle with me no more. For otherwise
We are no longer friends. And so, farewell!

[*Exit.*

HYPOLITO.

Now what a coil is here! The Avenging Child
Hunting the traitor Quadros to his death,
And the great Moor Calaynos, when he rode
To Paris for the ears of Oliver,
Were nothing to him! O hot-headed youth!
But come; we will not follow. Let us join
The crowd that pours into the Prado. There

We shall find merrier company ; I see

The Marialonzos and the Almavivas,

And fifty fans, that beckon me already.   [*Exeunt.*

SCENE IV.

PRECIOSA'S *chamber.   She is sitting, with a book in her
hand, near a table, on which are flowers.   A bird sing-
ing in its cage.   The* COUNT OF LARA *enters behind
unperceived.*

PRECIOSA (*reads*).

All are sleeping, weary heart !

Thou, thou only sleepless art !

Heigho ! I wish Victorian were here.

I know not what it is makes me so restless !

(*The bird sings.*)

Thou little prisoner with thy motley coat,

That from thy vaulted, wiry dungeon singest,

Like thee I am a captive, and, like thee,

I have a gentle gaoler.   Lack-a-day !

All are sleeping, weary heart!
Thou, thou only sleepless art!
All this throbbing, all this aching,
Evermore shall keep thee waking,
For a heart in sorrow breaking
Thinketh ever of its smart!

Thou speakest truly, poet! and methinks
More hearts are breaking in this world of ours
Than one would say.   In distant villages
And solitudes remote, where winds have wafted
The barbed seeds of love, or birds of passage
Scattered them in their flight, do they take
    root,
And grow in silence, and in silence perish.
Who hears the falling of the forest leaf?
Or who takes note of every flower that dies?
Heigho! I wish Victorian would come.
Dolores!
  (*Turns to lay down her book, and perceives the* COUNT.)
    Ha!

LARA.

Señora, pardon me !

PRECIOSA.

How 's this ?   Dolores !

LARA.

Pardon me ――――

PRECIOSA.

Dolores !

LARA.

Be not alarmed ; I found no one in waiting.
If I have been too bold ――――

PRECIOSA (*turning her back upon him*).

You are too bold !

Retire ! retire, and leave me !

LARA.

My dear lady,

First hear me !   I beseech you, let me speak !
'T is for your good I come.

PRECIOSA (*turning toward him with indignation*).

Begone !   Begone !

You are the Count of Lara, but your deeds
Would make the statues of your ancestors
Blush on their tombs!   Is it Castilian honor,
Is it Castilian pride, to steal in here
Upon a friendless girl, to do her wrong?
O shame! shame! shame! that you, a nobleman,
Should be so little noble in your thoughts
As to send jewels here to win my love,
And think to buy my honor with your gold!
I have no words to tell you how I scorn you!
Begone!   The sight of you is hateful to me!
Begone, I say!

LARA.

Be calm ; I will not harm you.

PRECIOSA.

Because you dare not.

LARA.

I dare any thing!
Therefore beware!   You are deceived in me.
In this false world, we do not always know

Who are our friends and who our enemies.
We all have enemies, and all need friends.
Even you, fair Preciosa, here at court
Have foes, who seek to wrong you.

PRECIOSA.

If to this
I owe the honor of the present visit,
You might have spared the coming.   Having
  spoken,
Once more I beg you, leave me to myself.

LARA.

I thought it but a friendly part to tell you
What strange reports are current here in town.
For my own self, I do not credit them ;
But there are many who, not knowing you,
Will lend a readier ear.

PRECIOSA.

There was no need
That you should take upon yourself the duty
Of telling me these tales.

LARA.

Malicious tongues

Are ever busy with your name.

PRECIOSA.

Alas!

I have no protectors.   I am a poor girl,

Exposed to insults and unfeeling jests.

They wound me, yet I cannot shield myself.

I give no cause for these reports.   I live

Retired; am visited by none.

LARA.

By none?

O, then, indeed, you are much wronged!

PRECIOSA.

How mean you?

LARA.

Nay, nay; I will not wound your gentle soul

By the report of idle tales.

PRECIOSA.

Speak out!

What are these idle tales? You need not spare me.

LARA.

I will deal frankly with you.   Pardon me ;
This window, as I think, looks toward the street,
And this into the Prado, does it not ?
In yon high house, beyond the garden wall, —
You see the roof there just above the trees, —
There lives a friend, who told me yesterday,
That on a certain night, — be not offended
If I too plainly speak, — he saw a man
Climb to your chamber window.   You are silent !
I would not blame you, being young and fair ——

(*He tries to embrace her.   She starts back, and draws a
dagger from her bosom.*)

PRECIOSA.

Beware ! beware ! I am a Gipsy girl !
Lay not your hand upon me.   One step nearer
And I will strike !

LARA.

        Pray you, put up that dagger.
Fear not.

PRECIOSA.

I do not fear.   I have a heart
In whose strength I can trust.

LARA.

Listen to me.
I come here as your friend, — I am your friend, —
And by a single word can put a stop
To all those idle tales, and make your name
Spotless as lilies are.   Here on my knees,
Fair Preciosa ! on my knees I swear,
I love you even to madness, and that love
Has driven me to break the rules of custom,
And force myself unasked into your presence.

(VICTORIAN *enters behind.*)

PRECIOSA.

Rise, Count of Lara !   That is not the place
For such as you are.   It becomes you not
To kneel before me.   I am strangely moved
To see one of your rank thus low and humbled ;
For your sake I will put aside all anger,

All unkind feeling, all dislike, and speak
In gentleness, as most becomes a woman,
And as my heart now prompts me.   I no more
Will hate you, for all hate is painful to me.
But if, without offending modesty
And that reserve which is a woman's glory,
I may speak freely, I will teach my heart
To love you.

LARA.

O sweet angel !

PRECIOSA.

Ay, in truth,
Far better than you love yourself or me.

LARA.

Give me some sign of this, — the slightest token.
Let me but kiss your hand !

PRECIOSA.

Nay, come no nearer.
The words I utter are its sign and token.
Misunderstand me not !   Be not deceived !

The love wherewith I love you is not such
As you would offer me. For you come here
To take from me the only thing I have,
My honor. You are wealthy, you have friends
And kindred, and a thousand pleasant hopes
That fill your heart with happiness ; but I
Am poor, and friendless, having but one treasure,
And you would take that from me, and for what ?
To flatter your own vanity, and make me
What you would most despise. O Sir, such love,
That seeks to harm me, cannot be true love.
Indeed it cannot. But my love for you
Is of a different kind. It seeks your good.
It is a holier feeling. It rebukes
Your earthly passion, your unchaste desires,
And bids you look into your heart, and see
How you do wrong that better nature in you,
And grieve your soul with sin.

LARA.

I swear to you,

I would not harm you ; I would only love you.

I would not take your honor, but restore it,

And in return I ask but some slight mark

Of your affection.   If indeed you love me,

As you confess you do, O let me thus

With this embrace ——

VICTORIAN (*rushing forward*).

        Hold ! hold ! This is too much.

What means this outrage ?

LARA.

        First, what right have you

To question thus a nobleman of Spain ?

VICTORIAN.

I too am noble, and you are no more !

Out of my sight !

LARA.

        Are you the master here ?

VICTORIAN.

Ay, here and elsewhere, when the wrong of others

Gives me the right !

PRECIOSA (*to* LARA).

Go ! I beseech you, go !

VICTORIAN.

I shall have business with you, Count, anon !

LARA.

You cannot come too soon !   [*Exit.*

PRECIOSA.

Victorian !

O we have been betrayed !

VICTORIAN.

Ha ! ha ! betrayed !

'T is I have been betrayed, not we ! — not we !

PRECIOSA.

Dost thou imagine ——

VICTORIAN.

I imagine nothing ;

I see how 't is thou whilest the time away

When I am gone !

PRECIOSA.

O speak not in that tone !

It wounds me deeply.

VICTORIAN.

'T was not meant to flatter.

PRECIOSA.

Too well thou knowest the presence of that man
Is hateful to me !

VICTORIAN.

Yet I saw thee stand
And listen to him, when he told his love.

PRECIOSA.

I did not heed his words.

VICTORIAN.

Indeed thou didst,
And answeredst them with love.

PRECIOSA.

Hadst thou heard all ——

VICTORIAN.

I heard enough.

PRECIOSA.

Be not so angry with me.

VICTORIAN.

I am not angry ; I am very calm.

PRECIOSA.

If thou wilt let me speak ——

VICTORIAN.

Nay, say no more.

I know too much already.   Thou art false !

I do not like these Gipsy marriages !

Where is the ring I gave thee ?

PRECIOSA.

In my casket.

VICTORIAN.

There let it rest ! I would not have thee wear it !

I thought thee spotless, and thou art polluted !

PRECIOSA.

I call the Heavens to witness ——

VICTORIAN.

Nay, nay, nay !

Take not the name of Heaven upon thy lips !

They are forsworn !

PRECIOSA.

Victorian ! dear Victorian !

25

VICTORIAN.

I gave up all for thee ; myself, my fame,
My hopes of fortune, ay, my very soul !
And thou hast been my ruin !   Now, go on !
Laugh at my folly with thy paramour,
And, sitting on the Count of Lara's knee,
Say what a poor, fond fool Victorian was !

(*He casts her from him and rushes out.*)

PRECIOSA.

And this from thee !

(*Scene closes.*)

SCENE V.

The COUNT OF LARA'S *rooms.   Enter the* COUNT.

LARA.

There 's nothing in this world so sweet as love,
And next to love the sweetest thing is hate !
I 've learned to hate, and therefore am revenged.
A silly girl to play the prude with me !
The fire that I have kindled ——

(*Enter* FRANCISCO.)

Well, Francisco,
What tidings from Don Juan ?

FRANCISCO.

Good, my lord ;
He will be present.

LARA.

And the Duke of Lermos ?

FRANCISCO.

Was not at home.

LARA.

How with the rest ?

FRANCISCO.

I 've found
The men you wanted.   They will all be there,
And at the given signal raise a whirlwind
Of such discordant noises, that the dance
Must cease for lack of music.

LARA.

Bravely done.

Ah! little dost thou dream, sweet Preciosa,
What lies in wait for thee. Sleep shall not close
Thine eyes this night! Give me my cloak and
   sword.   [*Exeunt*

SCENE VI.

A retired spot beyond the city gates. Enter VICTORIAN
and HYPOLITO.

VICTORIAN.

O shame! O shame! Why do I walk abroad
By daylight, when the very sunshine mocks me,
And voices, and familiar sights and sounds
Cry,"Hide thyself"! O what a thin partition
Doth shut out from the curious world the knowl-
   edge
Of evil deeds that have been done in darkness!
Disgrace has many tongues. My fears are win-
   dows,
Through which all eyes seem gazing. Every face

Expresses some suspicion of my shame,
And in derision seems to smile at me !

HYPOLITO.

Did I not caution thee ?   Did I not tell thee
I was but half persuaded of her virtue ?

VICTORIAN.

And yet, Hypolito, we may be wrong,
We may be over-hasty in condemning !
The Count of Lara is a cursed villain.

HYPOLITO.

And therefore is she cursed, loving him.

VICTORIAN.

She does not love him !   'T is for gold ! for
    gold !

HYPOLITO.

Ay, but remember, in the public streets
He shows a golden ring the Gipsy gave him,
A serpent with a ruby in its mouth.

VICTORIAN.

She had that ring from me !   God ! she is false !

But I will be revenged !   The hour is passed.
Where stays the coward ?

HYPOLITO.

      Nay, he is no coward ;
A villain, if thou wilt, but not a coward.
I 've seen him play with swords ; it is his pastime.
And therefore be not over-confident,
He 'll task thy skill anon. Look, here he comes.

   (*Enter* LARA, *followed by* FRÀNCISCO.)

LARA.

Good evening, gentlemen.

HYPOLITO.

     Good evening, Count.

LARA.

I trust I have not kept you long in waiting.

VICTORIAN.

Not long, and yet too long.   Are you prepared ?

LARA.

I am.

HYPOLITO.

  It grieves me much to see this quarrel

Between you, gentlemen.   Is there no way
Left open to accord this difference,
But you must make one with your swords ?

VICTORIAN.

No ! none !

I do entreat thee, dear Hypolito,
Stand not between me and my foe.   Too long
Our tongues have spoken.   Let these tongues of
    steel
End our debate.   Upon your guard, Sir Count !

(*They fight.*   VICTORIAN *disarms the* COUNT.)

Your life is mine ; and what shall now withhold me
From sending your vile soul to its account ?

LARA.

Strike ! strike !

VICTORIAN.

You are disarmed.   I will not kill you.
I will not murder you.   Take up your sword.

(FRANCISCO *hands the* COUNT *his sword, and* HYPOLITO
interposes.)

HYPOLITO.

Enough ! Let it end here ! The Count of Lara
Has shown himself a brave man, and Victorian
A generous one, as ever.   Now be friends.
Put up your swords ; for, to speak frankly to you,
Your cause of quarrel is too slight a thing
To move you to extremes.

LARA.

I am content.
I sought no quarrel.   A few hasty words,
Spoken in the heat of blood, have led to this.

VICTORIAN.

Nay, something more than that.

LARA.

I understand you.
Therein I did not mean to cross your path.
To me the door stood open, as to others.
But, had I known the girl belonged to you,
Never would I have sought to win her from you.
The truth stands now revealed ; she has been false
To both of us.

VICTORIAN.

Ay, false as hell itself!

LARA.

In truth I did not seek her ; she sought me ;
And told me how to win her, telling me
The hours when she was oftenest left alone.

VICTORIAN.

Say, can you prove this to me ?   O, pluck out
These awful doubts, that goad me into madness!
Let me know all ! all ! all !

LARA.

You shall know all.
Here is my page, who was the messenger
Between us.   Question him.   Was it not so,
Francisco ?

FRANCISCO.

Ay, my lord.

LARA.

If farther proof
Is needful, I have here a ring she gave me.

VICTORIAN.

Pray let me see that ring !   It is the same !

(*Throws it upon the ground, and tramples upon it.*)

Thus may she perish who once wore that ring !

Thus do I spurn her from me ; do thus trample

Her memory in the dust !   O Count of Lara,

We both have been abused, been much abused !

I thank you for your courtesy and frankness.

Though, like the surgeon's hand, yours gave me

>   pain,

Yet it has cured my blindness, and I thank you.

I now can see the folly I have done,

Though 't is, alas ! too late.   So fare you well !

To-night I leave this hateful town for ever.

Regard me as your friend. Once more, farewell !

HYPOLITO.

Farewell, Sir Count.

>   [*Exeunt* VICTORIAN *and* HYPOLITO.

LARA.

>   Farewell ! farewell !

Thus have I cleared the field of my worst foe !
I have none else to fear ; the fight is done,
The citadel is stormed, the victory won !

[*Exit with* FRANCISCO.

SCENE VII.

A lane in the suburbs. Night. Enter CRUZADO *and*
BARTOLOMÉ.

CRUZADO.

And so, Bartolomé, the expedition failed. But
where wast thou for the most part ?

BARTOLOMÉ.

In the Guadarrama mountains, near San Ilde-
fonso.

CRUZADO.

And thou bringest nothing back with thee ?
Didst thou rob no one ?

BARTOLOMÉ.

There was no one to rob, save a party of students from Segovia, who looked as if they would rob us ; and a jolly little friar, who had nothing in his pockets but a missal and a loaf of bread.

CRUZADO.

Pray, then, what brings thee back to Madrid ?

BARTOLOMÉ.

First tell me what keeps thee here ?

CRUZADO.

Preciosa.

BARTOLOMÉ.

And she brings me back.   Hast thou forgotten thy promise ?

CRUZADO.

The two years are not passed yet.   Wait patiently.   The girl shall be thine.

BARTOLOMÉ.

I hear she has a Busné lover.

CRUZADO.

That is nothing.

BARTOLOMÉ.

I do not like it.   I hate him, — the son of a
Busné harlot.   He goes in and out, and speaks
with her alone, and I must stand aside, and wait
his pleasure.

CRUZADO.

Be patient, I say.   Thou shalt have thy re
venge.   When the time comes, thou shalt way-
lay him.

BARTOLOMÉ.

Meanwhile, show me her house.

CRUZADO.

Come this way.   But thou wilt not find her.
She dances at the play to-night.

BARTOLOMÉ.

No matter.   Show me the house.   [*Exeunt.*

SCENE VIII.

*The Theatre.   The orchestra plays the cachucha.   Sound
of castanets behind the scenes.   The curtain rises, and
discovers* PRECIOSA *in the attitude of commencing the
dance.   The cachucha.   Tumult; hisses; cries of "Bra-
va!" and "Afuera!"   She falters and pauses.   The
music stops.   General confusion.* PRECIOSA *faints.*

SCENE IX.

The COUNT OF LARA'S *chambers.* LARA *and his friends
at supper.*

LARA.

So, Caballeros, once more many thanks !
You have stood by me bravely in this matter.
Pray fill your glasses.

DON JUAN.

Did you mark, Don Luis,
How pale she looked, when first the noise began,

And then stood still, with her large eyes dilated !
Her nostrils spread ! her lips apart ! her bosom
Tumultuous as the sea !

DON LUIS.

I pitied her.

LARA.

Her pride is humbled ; and this very night
I mean to visit her.

DON JUAN.

Will you serenade her ?

LARA.

No music ! no more music !

DON LUIS.

Why not music ?

It softens many hearts.

LARA.

Not in the humor
She now is in.   Music would madden her.

DON JUAN.

Try golden cymbals.

DON LUIS.

Yes, try Don Dinero ;

A mighty wooer is your Don Dinero.

LARA.

To tell the truth, then, I have bribed her maid.

But, Caballeros, you dislike this wine.

A bumper and away ; for the night wears.

A health to Preciosa !

(*They rise and drink.*)

ALL.

Preciosa.

LARA (*holding up his glass*).

Thou bright and flaming minister of Love !

Thou wonderful magician ! who hast stolen

My secret from me, and mid sighs of passion

Caught from my lips, with red and fiery tongue,

Her precious name !   O never more henceforth

Shall mortal lips press thine ; and never more

A mortal name be whispered in thine ear.

Go ! keep my secret !

(*Drinks and dashes the goblet down.*)

DON JUAN.

Ite ! missa est !

(*Scene closes.*)

SCENE X.

Street and garden wall. Night. Enter CRUZADO *and*
BARTOLOMÉ.

CRUZADO.

This is the garden wall, and above it, yonder,
is her house. The window in which thou seest
the light is her window. But we will not go in
now.

BARTOLOMÉ.

Why not ?

CRUZADO.

Because she is not at home.

BARTOLOMÉ.

No matter ; we can wait. But how is this ?
The gate is bolted. (*Sound of guitars and voices in*

26

a neighbouring street.) Hark ! There comes her lover with his infernal serenade ! Hark !

SONG.

Good night ! Good night, beloved !
I come to watch o'er thee !
To be near thee, — to be near thee,
Alone is peace for me.

Thine eyes are stars of morning,
Thy lips are crimson flowers !
Good night ! Good night, beloved,
While I count the weary hours.

CRUZADO.

They are not coming this way.

BARTOLOMÉ.

Wait, they begin again.

SONG (*coming nearer*).

Ah ! thou moon that shinest
Argent-clear above !
All night long enlighten
My sweet lady-love !
Moon that shinest,
All night long enlighten !

BARTOLOMÉ.

Woe be to him, if he comes this way!

CRUZADO.

Be quiet, they are passing down the street.

SONG (*dying away*).

The nuns in the cloister
  Sang to each other;
For so many sisters
  Is there not one brother!
Ay, for the partridge, mother!
  The cat has run away with the partridge!
Puss! puss! puss!

BARTOLOMÉ.

Follow that! follow that! Come with me.
Puss! puss!

(*Exeunt. On the opposite side enter the* COUNT OF LARA
  and gentlemen, with FRANCISCO.)

LARA.

The gate is fast. Over the wall, Francisco,
And draw the bolt. There, so, and so, and over.
Now, gentlemen, come in, and help me scale

Yon balcony. How now ? Her light still burns.
Move warily.   Make fast the gate, Francisco.

(*Exeunt.   Reënter* Cruzado *and* Bartolomé.)

BARTOLOMÉ.

They went in at the gate. Hark! I hear them
in the garden. (*Tries the gate.*)   Bolted again !
Vive Cristo !   Follow me over the wall.

(*They climb the wall.*)

SCENE XI.

Preciosa's *bed-chamber.   Midnight.   She is sleeping in
an arm-chair, in an undress.* Dolores *watching her.*

DOLORES.

She sleeps at last !

(*Opens the window and listens.*)

All silent in the street,
And in the garden.   Hark !

PRECIOSA (*in her sleep*).

I must go hence!

Give me my cloak!

DOLORES.

He comes! I hear his footsteps!

PRECIOSA.

Go tell them that I cannot dance to-night;
I am too ill! Look at me! See the fever
That burns upon my cheek! I must go hence.
I am too weak to dance.

(*Signal from the garden.*)

DOLORES (*from the window*).

Who 's there?

VOICE (*from below*).

A friend.

DOLORES.

I will undo the door. Wait till I come.

PRECIOSA.

I must go hence. I pray you do not harm me!
Shame! shame! to treat a feeble woman thus!

Be you but kind, I will do all things for you.

I 'm ready now, — give me my castanets.

Where is Victorian ?   Oh, those hateful lamps !

They glare upon me like an evil eye.

I cannot stay.   Hark ! how they mock at me !

They hiss at me like serpents ! Save me ! save me!

(She wakes.)

How late is it, Dolores ?

DOLORES.

It is midnight.

PRECIOSA.

We must be patient. Smooth this pillow for me.

(She sleeps again.   Noise from the garden, and voices.)

VOICE.

Muera !

ANOTHER VOICE.

O villains ! villains !

LARA.

So ! have at you !

VOICE.

Take that !

LARA.

O, I am wounded !

DOLORES (*shutting the window*).

Jesu Maria !

ACT III

SCENE I. *A cross-road through a wood.   In the back-
ground a distant village spire.* VICTORIAN *and* HYPO
LITO, *as travelling students, with guitars, sitting under
the trees.* HYPOLITO *plays and sings.*

SONG.

Ah, Love !

Perjured, false, treacherous Love !

Enemy

Of all that mankind may not rue !

Most untrue

To him who keeps most faith with thee.

Woe is me !

The falcon has the eyes of the dove.

Ah, Love !

Perjured, false, treacherous Love !

VICTORIAN.

Yes, Love is ever busy with his shuttle,

Is ever weaving into life's dull warp
Bright, gorgeous flowers and scenes Arcadian ;
Hanging our gloomy prison-house about
With tapestries, that make its walls dilate
In never-ending vistas of delight.

HYPOLITO.

Thinking to walk in those Arcadian pastures,
Thou hast run thy noble head against the wall.

SONG (*continued*).

Thy deceits
Give us clearly to comprehend,
Whither tend
All thy pleasures, all thy sweets !
They are cheats,
Thorns below and flowers above.
Ah, Love !
Perjured, false, treacherous Love!

VICTORIAN.

A very pretty song.   I thank thee for it.

HYPOLITO.

It suits thy case.

VICTORIAN.

Indeed, I think it does.

What wise man wrote it?

HYPOLITO.

Lopez Maldonado.

VICTORIAN.

In truth, a pretty song.

HYPOLITO.

With much truth in it.

I hope thou wilt profit by it ; and in earnest
Try to forget this lady of thy love.

VICTORIAN.

I will forget her !   All dear recollections
Pressed in my heart, like flowers within a book,
Shall be torn out, and scattered to the winds !
I will forget her !   But perhaps hereafter,
When she shall learn how heartless is the world,
A voice within her will repeat my name,
And she will say, " He was indeed my friend ! "
O, would I were a soldier, not a scholar,

That the loud march, the deafening beat of drums,
The shattering blast of the brass-throated trumpet,
The din of arms, the onslaught and the storm,
And a swift death, might make me deaf for ever
To the upbraidings of this foolish heart !

HYPOLITO.

Then let that foolish heart upbraid no more !
To conquer love, one need but will 'to conquer.

VICTORIAN.

Yet, good Hypolito, it is in vain
I throw into Oblivion's sea the sword
That pierces me ; for, like Excalibar,
With gemmed and flashing hilt, it will not sink.
There rises from below a hand that grasps it,
And waves it in the air ; and wailing voices
Are heard along the shore.

HYPOLITO.

     And yet at last
Down sank Excalibar to rise no more.
This is not well.   In truth, it vexes me.

Instead of whistling to the steeds of Time,
To make them jog on merrily with life's burden,
Like a dead weight thou hangest on the wheels.
Thou art too young, too full of lusty health
To talk of dying.

VICTORIAN.

Yet I fain would die !
To go through life, unloving and unloved ;
To feel that thirst and hunger of the soul
We cannot still ; that longing, that wild impulse,
And struggle after something we have not
And cannot have ; the effort to be strong ;
And, like the Spartan boy, to smile, and smile,
While secret wounds do bleed beneath our cloaks ;
All this the dead feel not, — the dead alone !
Would I were with them !

HYPOLITO.

We shall all be soon.

VICTORIAN.

It cannot be too soon ; for I am weary

Of the bewildering masquerade of Life,
Where strangers walk as friends, and friends as
    strangers ;
Where whispers overheard betray false hearts ;
And through the mazes of the crowd we chase
Some form of loveliness, that smiles, and beckons,
And cheats us with fair words, only to leave us
A mockery and a jest ; maddened, — confused, —
Not knowing friend from foe.

HYPOLITO.

               Why seek to know ?
Enjoy the merry shrove-tide of thy youth !
Take each fair mask for what it gives itself,
Nor strive to look beneath it.

VICTORIAN.

               I confess,
That were the wiser part.   But Hope no longer
Comforts my soul.   I am a wretched man,
Much like a poor and shipwrecked mariner,
Who, struggling to climb up into the boat,

Has both his bruised and bleeding hands cut off,
And sinks again into the weltering sea,
Helpless and hopeless !

HYPOLITO.

Yet thou shalt not perish.
The strength of thine own arm is thy salvation.
Above thy head, through rifted clouds, there shines
A glorious star.   Be patient.   Trust thy star !

(*Sound of a village bell in the distance.*)

VICTORIAN.

Ave Maria !   I hear the sacristan
Ringing the chimes from yonder village belfry !
A solemn sound, that echoes far and wide
Over the red roofs of the cottages,
And bids the laboring hind a-field, the shepherd,
Guarding his flock, the lonely muleteer,
And all the crowd in village streets, stand still,
And breathe a prayer unto the blessed Virgin !

HYPOLITO.

Amen ! amen !   Not half a league from hence
The village lies.

VICTORIAN.

This path will lead us to it,
Over the wheat fields, where the shadows sail
Across the running sea, now green, now blue,
And, like an idle mariner on the main,
Whistles the quail. Come, let us hasten on.

[*Exeunt.*

SCENE II.

*Public square in the village of Guadarrama. The Ave
Maria still tolling. A crowd of villagers, with their
hats in their hands, as if in prayer. In front, a group
of Gipsies. The bell rings a merrier peal. A Gipsy
dance. Enter* PANCHO, *followed by* PEDRO CRESPO.

PANCHO.

Make room, ye vagabonds and Gipsy thieves!
Make room for the Alcalde and for me!

PEDRO CRESPO.

Keep silence all! I have an edict here
From our most gracious lord, the King of Spain,

Jerusalem, and the Canary Islands,

Which I shall publish in the market-place.

Open your ears and listen !

(*Enter the* PADRE CURA *at the door of his cottage.*)

Padre Cura,

Good day ! and, pray you, hear this edict read.

PADRE CURA.

Good day, and God be with you!   Pray, what

is it ?

PEDRO CRESPO.

An act of banishment against the Gipsies !

(*Agitation and murmurs in the crowd.*)

PANCHO.

Silence !

PEDRO CRESPO (*reads*).

" I hereby order and command,

That the Egyptian and Chaldean strangers,

Known by the name of Gipsies, shall henceforth

Be banished from the realm, as vagabonds

And beggars ; and if, after seventy days,

Any be found within our kingdom's bounds,
They shall receive a hundred lashes each;
The second time, shall have their ears cut off;
The third, be slaves for life to him who takes them,
Or burnt as heretics. Signed, I, the King."
Vile miscreants and creatures unbaptized!
You hear the law! Obey and disappear!

PANCHO.

And if in seventy days you are not gone,
Dead or alive I make you all my slaves.

(*The Gipsies go out in confusion, showing signs of fear
and discontent.* PANCHO *follows.*)

PADRE CURA.

A righteous law! A very righteous law!
Pray you, sit down.

PEDRO CRESPO.

I thank you heartily.

(*They seat themselves on a bench at the* PADRE CURA'S
*door. Sound of guitars heard at a distance, approach-
ing during the dialogue which follows.*)

27

A very righteous judgment, as you say.
Now tell me, Padre Cura,—you know all things,—
How came these Gipsies into Spain ?

PADRE CURA.

Why, look you ;
They came with Hercules from Palestine,
And hence are thieves and vagrants, Sir Alcalde,
As the Simoniacs from Simon Magus.
And, look you, as Fray Jayme Bleda says,
There are a hundred marks to prove a Moor
Is not a Christian, so 't is with the Gipsies.
They never marry, never go to mass,
Never baptize their children, nor keep Lent,
Nor see the inside of a church, — nor — nor —

PEDRO CRESPO.

Good reasons, good, substantial reasons all !
No matter for the other ninety-five.
They should be burnt, I see it plain enough,
They should be burnt.

(*Enter* Victorian *and* Hypolito *playing.*)

PADRE CURA.

And pray, whom have we here ?

PEDRO CRESPO.

More vagrants! By Saint Lazarus, more vagrants!

HYPOLITO.

Good evening, gentlemen ! Is this Guadarrama ?

PADRE CURA.

Yes, Guadarrama, and good evening to you.

HYPOLITO.

We seek the Padre Cura of the village ;

And, judging from your dress and reverend mien,

You must be he.

PADRE CURA.

I am. Pray, what 's your pleasure ?

HYPOLITO.

We are poor students, travelling in vacation.

You know this mark ?

(*Touching the wooden spoon in his hat-band.*)

PADRE CURA (*joyfully*).

Ay, know it, and have worn it.

PEDRO CRESPO (*aside*).

Soup-eaters! by the mass! The worst of vagrants!
And there 's no law against them. Sir, your ser-
vant.   [*Exit.*

PADRE CURA.

Your servant, Pedro Crespo.

HYPOLITO.

Padre Cura,
From the first moment I beheld your face,
I said within myself, " This is the man! "
There is a certain something in your looks,
A certain scholar-like and studious something, —
You understand, — which cannot be mistaken;
Which marks you as a very learned man,
In fine, as one of us.

VICTORIAN (*aside*).

What impudence !

HYPOLITO.

As we approached, I said to my companion,
" That is the Padre Cura; mark my words! "

Meaning your Grace. " The other man," said I,
" Who sits so awkwardly upon the bench,
Must be the sacristan."

PADRE CURA.

            Ah ! said you so ?
Why, that was Pedro Crespo, the alcalde !

HYPOLITO.

Indeed ! you much astonish me !   His air
Was not so full of dignity and grace
As an alcalde's should be.

PADRE CURA.

           That is true.
He is out of humor with some vagrant Gipsies,
Who have their camp here in the neighbourhood
There is nothing so undignified as anger.

HYPOLITO.

The Padre Cura will excuse our boldness,
If, from his well-known hospitality,
We crave a lodging for the night.

PADRE CURA.

I pray you!

You do me honor! I am but too happy

To have such guests beneath my humble roof.

It is not often that I have occasion

To speak with scholars ; and *Emollit mores,*

Nec sinit esse feros, Cicero says.

HYPOLITO.

'T is Ovid, is it not ?

PADRE CURA.

No, Cicero.

HYPOLITO.

Your Grace is right. You are the better scholar.

Now what a dunce was I to think it Ovid!

But hang me if it is not ! (*Aside.*)

PADRE CURA.

Pass this way.

He was a very great man, was Cicero !

Pray you, go in, go in ! no ceremony. [*Exeunt.*

SCENE III.

A room in the PADRE CURA'S *house. Enter the* PADRE *and* HYPOLITO.

PADRE CURA.

So then, Señor, you come from Alcalá.
I am glad to hear it.   It was there I studied.

HYPOLITO.

And left behind an honored name, no doubt.
How may I call your Grace ?

PADRE CURA.

Gerónimo

De Santillana, at your Honor's service.

HYPOLITO.

Descended from the Marquis Santillana ?
From the distinguished poet ?

PADRE CURA.

From the Marquis,

Not from the poet.

HYPOLITO.

Why, they were the same.
Let me embrace you! O some lucky star
Has brought me hither! Yet once more!—once
    more!
Your name is ever green in Alcalá,
And our professor, when we are unruly,
Will shake his hoary head, and say, " Alas!
It was not so in Santillana's time!"

PADRE CURA.

I did not think my name remembered there.

HYPOLITO.

More than remembered ; it is idolized.

PADRE CURA.

Of what professor speak you ?

HYPOLITO.

                    Timoneda.

PADRE CURA.

I don't remember any Timoneda.

HYPOLITO.

A grave and sombre man, whose beetling brow

O'erhangs the rushing current of his speech
As rocks o'er rivers hang.   Have you forgotten?

PADRE CURA.

Indeed, I have.   O, those were pleasant days,
Those college days!   I ne'er shall see the like!
I had not buried then so many hopes!
I had not buried then so many friends!
I 've turned my back on what was then before me;
And the bright faces of my young companions
Are wrinkled like my own, or are no more.
Do you remember Cueva?

HYPOLITO.

Cueva?   Cueva?

PADRE CURA.

Fool that I am!   He was before your time.
You 're a mere boy, and I am an old man.

HYPOLITO.

I should not like to try my strength with you.

PADRE CURA.

Well, well.   But I forget; you must be hungry.
Martina! ho! Martina!   'T is my niece.

(*Enter* Martina.)

HYPOLITO.

You may be proud of such a niece as that.

I wish I had a niece. *Emollit mores.* (*Aside.*)

He was a very great man, was Cicero!

Your servant, fair Martina.

MARTINA.

Servant, sir.

PADRE CURA.

This gentleman is hungry. See thou to it.

Let us have supper.

MARTINA.

'T will be ready soon.

PADRE CURA.

And bring a bottle of my Val-de-Peñas

Out of the cellar. Stay; I 'll go myself.

Pray you, Señor, excuse me. [*Exit.*

HYPOLITO.

Hist! Martina!

One word with you. Bless me! what handsome

eyes!

To-day there have been Gipsies in the village.
Is it not so?

MARTINA.

There have been Gipsies here.

HYPOLITO.

Yes, and they told your fortune.

MARTINA (*embarrassed*).

Told my fortune?

HYPOLITO.

Yes, yes; I know they did.   Give me your hand.
I 'll tell you what they said.   They said, — they
    said,
The shepherd boy that loved you was a clown,
And him you should not marry.   Was it not?

MARTINA (*surprised.*)

How know you that?

HYPOLITO.

O, I know more than that.
What a soft, little hand!   And then they said,
A cavalier from court, handsome, and tall

And rich, should come one day to marry you,

And you should be a lady.   Was it not ?

He has arrived, the handsome cavalier.

(*Tries to kiss her.   She runs off.   Enter* VICTORIAN, *with a letter.*)

VICTORIAN.

The muleteer has come.

HYPOLITO.

So soon ?

VICTORIAN.

I found him

Sitting at supper by the tavern door,

And, from a pitcher that he held aloft

His whole arm's length, drinking the blood-red wine.

HYPOLITO.

What news from Court ?

VICTORIAN.

He brought this letter only.   (*Reads.*)

O cursed perfidy !   Why did I let

That lying tongue deceive me ! Preciosa,

Sweet Preciosa ! how art thou avenged !

HYPOLITO.

What news is this, that makes thy cheek turn

pale,

And thy hand tremble ?

VICTORIAN.

O, most infamous !

The Count of Lara is a damnéd villain !

HYPOLITO.

That is no news, forsooth.

VICTORIAN.

He strove in vain

To steal from me the jewel of my soul,

The love of Preciosa.   Not succeeding,

He swore to be revenged ; and set on foot

A plot to ruin her, which has succeeded.

She has been hissed and hooted from the stage,

Her reputation stained by slanderous lies

Too foul to speak of ; and, once more a beggar,

She roams a wanderer over God's green earth,
Housing with Gipsies!

HYPOLITO.

To renew again
The Age of Gold, and make the shepherd swains
Desperate with love, like Gaspar Gil's Diana.
Redit et Virgo!

VICTORIAN.

Dear Hypolito,
How have I wronged that meek, confiding heart!
I will go seek for her ; and with my tears
Wash out the wrong I 've done her !

HYPOLITO.

O beware '
Act not that folly o'er again.

VICTORIAN.

Ay, folly,
Delusion, madness, call it what thou wilt,
I will confess my weakness, — I still love her !
Still fondly love her !

(*Enter the* PADRE CURA.)

HYPOLITO.

Tell us, Padre Cura,
Who are these Gipsies in the neighbourhood ?

PADRE CURA.

Beltran Cruzado and his crew.

VICTORIAN.

Kind Heaven,
I thank thee !   She is found ! is found again !

HYPOLITO.

And have they with them a pale, beautiful girl,
Called Preciosa ?

PADRE CURA.

Ay, a pretty girl.
The gentleman seems moved.

HYPOLITO.

Yes, moved with hunger ;
He is half famished with this long day's journey.

PADRE CURA.

Then, pray you, come this way.   The supper
waits.   [*Exeunt.*

SCENE IV.

A post-house on the road to Segovia, not far from the village' of Guadarrama. Enter CHISPA, *cracking a whip and singing the Cachucha.*

CHISPA.

Halloo! Don Fulano! Let us have horses, and quickly. Alas, poor Chispa! what a dog's life dost thou lead! I thought, when I left my old master Victorian, the student, to serve my new master Don Carlos, the gentleman, that I, too, should lead the life of a gentleman; should go to bed early, and get up late. For when the abbot plays cards, what can you expect of the friars? But, in running away from the thunder, I have run into the lightning. Here I am in hot chase after my master and his Gipsy girl. And a good beginning of the week it is, as he said who was hanged on Monday morning.

(*Enter* DON CARLOS.)

DON CARLOS.

Are not the horses ready yet ?

CHISPA.

I should think not, for the hostler seems to be asleep. Ho! within there! Horses! horses! horses! (*He knocks at the gate with his whip, and enter* MOSQUITO, *putting on his jacket.*)

MOSQUITO.

Pray, have a little patience. I 'm not a musket.

CHISPA.

Health and pistareens! I 'm glad to see you come on dancing, padre! Pray, what 's the news ?

MOSQUITO.

You cannot have fresh horses ; because there are none.

CHISPA.

Cachiporra! Throw that bone to another dog. Do I look like your aunt ?

MOSQUITO.

No ; she has a beard.

28

CHISPA.

Go to ! go to !

MOSQUITO.

Are you from Madrid ?

CHISPA.

Yes ; and going to Estramadura. Get us horses.

MOSQUITO.

What 's the news at Court ?

CHISPA.

Why, the latest news is, that I am going to set
up a coach, and I have already bought the whip.

(*Strikes him round the legs.*)

MOSQUITO.

Oh ! oh ! you hurt me !

DON CARLOS.

Enough of this folly.   Let us have horses.
(*Gives money to* MOSQUITO.)   It is almost dark ; and
we are in haste.   But tell me, has a band of Gip-
sies passed this way of late ?

MOSQUITO.

Yes ; and they are still in the neighbourhood.

DON CARLOS.

And where ?

MOSQUITO.

Across the fields yonder, in the woods near
Guadarrama.   [*Exit.*

DON CARLOS.

Now this is lucky. We will visit the Gipsy
camp.

CHISPA.

Are you not afraid of the evil eye ? Have
you a stag's horn with you ?

DON CARLOS.

Fear not. We will pass the night at the village.

CHISPA.

And sleep like the Squires of Hernan Daza,
nine under one blanket.

DON CARLOS.

I hope we may find the Preciosa among them.

CHISPA.

Among the Squires ?

DON CARLOS.

No ; among the Gipsies, blockhead !

CHISPA.

I hope we may ; for we are giving ourselves
trouble enough on her account.   Don't you think
so ? However, there is no catching trout without
wetting one's trowsers. Yonder come the horses.

[*Exeunt.*

SCENE V.

*The Gipsy camp in the forest.   Night.   Gipsies working
at a forge.   Others playing cards by the fire-light.*

GIPSIES (*at the forge sing*).

On the top of a mountain I stand,
With a crown of red gold in my hand,
Wild Moors come trooping over the lea,
O how from their fury shall I flee, flee, flee!
O how from their fury shall I flee?

FIRST GIPSY (*playing*).

Down with your John-Dorados, my pigeon.

Down with your John-Dorados, and let us make
an end.

GIPSIES (*at the forge sing*).

Loud sang the Spanish cavalier,
And thus his ditty ran;
God send the Gipsy lassie here,
And not the Gipsy man.

FIRST GIPSY (*playing*).

There you are in your morocco .

SECOND GIPSY.

One more game. The Alcalde's doves against
the Padre Cura's new moon.

FIRST GIPSY.

Have at you, Chirelin.

GIPSIES (*at the forge sing*).

At midnight, when the moon began
To show her silver flame,
There came to him no Gipsy man,
The Gipsy lassie came.

(*Enter* BELTRAN CRUZADO.)

CRUZADO.

Come hither, Murcigalleros and Rastilleros;
leave work, leave play; listen to your orders for
the night.   (*Speaking to the right.*)   You will get
you to the village, mark you, by the stone cross.

GIPSIES.

Ay!

CRUZADO (*to the left*).

And you, by the pole with the hermit's head
upon it.

GIPSIES.

Ay!

CRUZADO.

As soon as you see the planets are out, in with
you, and be busy with the ten commandments,
under the sly, and Saint Martin asleep.   D' ye
hear?

GIPSIES.

Ay!

CRUZADO.

Keep your lanterns open, and, if you see a

goblin or a papagayo, take to your trampers.
"Vineyards and Dancing John" is the word.
Am I comprehended ?

GIPSIES.

Ay! ay!

CRUZADO.

Away, then!

(*Exeunt severally.* CRUZADO *walks up the stage, and disappears among the trees. Enter* PRECIOSA.)

PRECIOSA.

How strangely gleams through the gigantic trees
The red light of the forge! Wild, beckoning
    shadows
Stalk through the forest, ever and anon
Rising and bending with the flickering flame,
Then flitting into darkness! So within me
Strange hopes and fears do beckon to each other,
My brightest hopes giving dark fears a being
As the light does the shadow. Woe is me!
How still it is about me, and how lonely!

(Bartolomé *rushes in.*)

BARTOLOMÉ.

Ho ! Preciosa !

PRECIOSA.

O, Bartolomé !

Thou here ?

BARTOLOMÉ.

Lo ! I am here.

PRECIOSA.

Whence comest thou ?

BARTOLOMÉ.

From the rough ridges of the wild Sierra,
From caverns in the rocks, from hunger, thirst,
And fever ! Like a wild wolf to the sheepfold
Come I for thee, my lamb.

PRECIOSA.

O touch me not !

The Count of Lara's blood is on thy hands !
The Count of Lara's curse is on thy soul !
Do not come near me ! Pray, begone from here !

Thou art in danger !   They have set a price
Upon thy head !

BARTOLOMÉ.

                    Ay, and I 've wandered long
Among the mountains ; and for many days
Have seen no human face, save the rough swine-
        herd's.
The wind and rain have been my sole companions.
I shouted to them from the rocks thy name,
And the loud echo sent it back to me,
Till I grew mad.   I could not stay from thee,
And I am here !   Betray me, if thou wilt.

PRECIOSA.

Betray thee ?   I betray thee ?

BARTOLOMÉ.

                        Preciosa !
I come for thee ! for thee I thus brave death !
Fly with me o'er the borders of this realm !
Fly with me !

PRECIOSA.

Speak of that no more. I cannot.
I am thine nc longer.

BARTOLOMÉ.

O, recall the time
When we were children ! how we played to-
      gether,
How we grew up together ; how we plighted
Our hearts unto each other, even in childhood !
Fulfil thy promise, for the hour has come.
I am hunted from the kingdom, like a wolf !
Fulfil thy promise.

PRECIOSA.

'T was my father's promise,
Not mine.   I never gave my heart to thee,
Nor promised thee my hand !

BARTOLOMÉ.

False tongue of woman !
And heart more false !

PRECIOSA.

Nay, listen unto me.

I will speak frankly.   I have never loved thee ;
I cannot love thee.   This is not my fault,
It is my destiny.   Thou art a man
Restless and violent.   What wouldst thou with me,
A feeble girl, who have not long to live,
Whose heart is broken ?   Seek another wife,
Better than I, and fairer ; and let not
Thy rash and headlong moods estrange her from
          thee.
Thou art unhappy in this hopeless passion.
I never sought thy love ; never did aught
To make thee love me.   Yet I pity thee,
And most of all I pity thy wild heart,
That hurries thee to crimes and deeds of blood.
Beware, beware of that.

BARTOLOMÉ.

For thy dear sake,
I will be gentle.   Thou shalt teach me patience.

PRECIOSA.

Then take this farewell, and depart in peace.

Thou must not linger here.

BARTOLOMÉ.

Come, come with me.

PRECIOSA.

Hark ! I hear footsteps.

BARTOLOMÉ.

I entreat thee, come !

PRECIOSA.

Away ! It is in vain.

BARTOLOMÉ.

Wilt thor not come ?

PRECIOSA.

Never !

BARTOLOMÉ.

Then woe, eternal woe, upon thee !

Thou shalt not be another's.   Thou shalt die.

[*Exit.*

PRECIOSA.

All holy angels keep me in this hour !

Spirit of her who bore me, look upon me!
Mother of God, the glorified, protect me!
Christ and the saints, be merciful unto me!
Yet why should I fear death? What is it to
        die?
To leave all disappointment, care, and sorrow,
To leave all falsehood, treachery, and unkindness,
All ignominy, suffering, and despair,
And be at rest for ever! O, dull heart,
Be of good cheer! When thou shalt cease to
        beat,
Then shalt thou cease to suffer and complain!

(*Enter* VICTORIAN *and* HYPOLITO *behind.*)

VICTORIAN.

'T is she! Behold, how beautiful she stands
Under the tent-like trees!

HYPOLITO.

                    A woodland nymph!

VICTORIAN.

I pray thee, stand aside. Leave me.

HYPOLITO.

Be wary.

Do not betray thyself too soon.

VICTORIAN (*disguising his voice*).

Hist! Gipsy!

PRECIOSA (*aside, with emotion*).

That voice! that voice from heaven! O speak
   again!
Who is it calls?

VICTORIAN.

A friend.

PRECIOSA (*aside*).

'T is he! 'T is he!
I thank thee, Heaven, that thou hast heard my
   prayer,
And sent me this protector! Now be strong,
Be strong, my heart! I must dissemble here.
False friend or true?

VICTORIAN.

A true friend to the true;
Fear not; come hither. So; can you tell fortunes?

PRECIOSA.

Not in the dark. Come nearer to the fire.
Give me your hand. It is not crossed, I see.

VICTORIAN (*putting a piece of gold into her hand*).
There is the cross.

PRECIOSA.

Is 't silver?

VICTORIAN.

No, 't is gold.

PRECIOSA.

There 's a fair lady at the Court, who loves you,
And for yourself alone.

VICTORIAN.

Fie! the old story!
Tell me a better fortune for my money;
Not this old woman's tale!

PRECIOSA.

You are passionate;
And this same passionate humor in your blood
Has marred your fortune. Yes; I see it now;

The line of life is crossed by many marks.

Shame ! shame !   O you have wronged the maid

  who loved you !

How could you do it ?

VICTORIAN.

      I never loved a maid ;

For she I loved was then a maid no more.

PRECIOSA.

How know you that ?

VICTORIAN.

     A little bird in the air

Whispered the secret.

PRECIOSA.

    There, take back your gold !

Your hand is cold, like a deceiver's hand !

There is no blessing in its charity !

Make her your wife, for you have been abused ;

And you shall mend your fortunes, mending hers.

VICTORIAN (aside).

How like an angel's speaks the tongue of woman,

When pleading in another's cause her own! ———
That is a pretty ring upon your finger.
Pray give it me.   (*Tries to take the ring.*)

PRECIOSA.

No ; never from my hand
Shall that be taken !

VICTORIAN.

Why, 't is but a ring.
I 'll give it back to you ; or, if I keep it,
Will give you gold to buy you twenty such.

PRECIOSA.

Why would you have this ring ?

VICTORIAN.

A traveller's fancy,
A whim, and nothing more.   I would fain keep it
As a memento of the Gipsy camp
In Guadarrama, and the fortune-teller
Who sent me back to wed a widowed maid.
Pray, let me have the ring.

PRECIOSA.

No, never ! never !

29

I will not part with it, even when I die ;
But bid my nurse fold my pale fingers thus,
That it may not fall from them.   'T is a token
Of a beloved friend, who is no more.

VICTORIAN.

How ? dead ?

PRECIOSA.

Yes ; dead to me ; and worse than dead.
He is estranged !   And yet I keep this ring.
I will rise with it from my grave hereafter,
To prove to him that I was never false.

VICTORIAN (*aside*).

Be still, my swelling heart ! one moment, still !
Why, 't is the folly of a love-sick girl.
Come, give it me, or I will say 't is mine,
And that you stole it.

PRECIOSA.

O, you will not dare
To utter such a fiendish lie !

VICTORIAN.

Not dare ?

Look in my face, and say if there is aught
I have not dared, I would not dare for thee !

(She rushes into his arms.)

PRECIOSA.

'T is thou ! 't is thou !   Yes ; yes ; my heart's
    elected !
My dearest-dear Victorian ! my soul's heaven !
Where hast thou been so long ?   Why didst thou
    leave me ?

VICTORIAN.

Ask me not now, my dearest Preciosa.
Let me forget we ever have been parted !

PRECIOSA.

Hadst thou not come ——

VICTORIAN.

                            I pray thee, do not chide me !

PRECIOSA.

I should have perished here among these Gipsies.

VICTORIAN.

Forgive me, sweet ! for what I made thee suffer.

Think'st thou this heart could feel a moment's joy,
Thou being absent ?   O, believe it not !
Indeed, since that sad hour I have not slept,
For thinking of the wrong I did to thee !
Dost thou forgive me ? Say, wilt thou forgive me ?

PRECIOSA.

I have forgiven thee.   Ere those words of anger
Were in the book of Heaven writ down against
        thee,
I had forgiven thee.

VICTORIAN.

                I 'm the veriest fool
That walks the earth, to have believed thee false
It was the Count of Lara ——

PRECIOSA.

                    That bad man
Has worked me harm enough.   Hast thou not
        heard ——

VICTORIAN.

I have heard all.   And yet speak on, speak on !

Let me but hear thy voice, and I am happy;
For every tone, like some sweet incantation,
Calls up the buried past to plead for me.
Speak, my beloved, speak into my heart,
Whatever fills and agitates thine own.

(*They walk aside.*)

HYPOLITO.

All gentle quarrels in the pastoral poets,
All passionate love scenes in the best romances,
All chaste embraces on the public stage,
All soft adventures, which the liberal stars
Have winked at, as the natural course of things,
Have been surpassed here by my friend, the student,
And this sweet Gipsy lass, fair Preciosa!

PRECIOSA.

Señor Hypolito! I kiss your hand.
Pray, shall I tell your fortune?

HYPOLITO.

Not to-night;

For, should you treat me as you did Victorian,
And send me back to marry maids forlorn,
My wedding day would last from now till Christ-
    mas.

CHISPA (*within*).

What ho! the Gipsies, ho! Beltran Cruzado!
Halloo! halloo! halloo! halloo!

(*Enters booted, with a whip and lantern.*)

VICTORIAN.

           What now?
Why such a fearful din? Hast thou been robbed?

CHISPA.

Ay, robbed and murdered; and good evening to
    you,
My worthy masters.

VICTORIAN.

        Speak; what brings thee here?

CHISPA (*to Preciosa*).

Good news from Court; good news! Beltran
    Cruzado,

The Count of the Calés, is not your father,
But your true father has returned to Spain
Laden with wealth.   You are no more a Gipsy

VICTORIAN.

Strange as a Moorish tale !

CHISPA.

                        And we have all
Been drinking at the tavern to your health,
As wells drink in November, when it rains.

VICTORIAN.

Where is the gentleman ?

CHISPA.

                        As the old song says,

His body is in Segovia,
His soul is in Madrid.

PRECIOSA.

Is this a dream ?   O, if it be a dream,
Let me sleep on, and do not wake me yet !
Repeat thy story !   Say I 'm not deceived !
Say that I do not dream !   I am awake ;

This is the Gipsy camp ; this is Victorian,
And this his friend, Hypolito ! Speak ! speak !
Let me not wake and find it all a dream !

VICTORIAN.

It is a dream, sweet child ! a waking dream,
A blissful certainty, a vision bright
Of that rare happiness, which even on earth
Heaven gives to those it loves. Now art thou rich,
As thou wast ever beautiful and good ;
And I am now the beggar.

PRECIOSA (*giving him her hand*).

I have still

A hand to give.

CHISPA (*aside*).

And I have two to take.

I 've heard my grandmother say, that Heaven
    gives almonds
To those who have no teeth. That 's nuts to crack.
I 've teeth to spare, but where shall I find al-
    monds ?

VICTORIAN.

What more of this strange story ?

CHISPA.

Nothing more.
Your friend, Don Carlos, is now at the village
Showing to Pedro Crespo, the Alcalde,
The proofs of what I tell you.   The old hag,
Who stole you in your childhood, has confessed ;
And probably they 'll hang her for the crime,
To make the celebration more complete.

VICTORIAN.

No ; let it be a day of general joy ;
Fortune comes well to all, that comes not late.
Now let us join Don Carlos.

HYPOLITO.

So farewell,
The student's wandering life !   Sweet serenades,
Sung under ladies' windows in the night,
And all that makes vacation beautiful !
To you, ye cloistered shades of Alcalá,

To you, ye radiant visions of romance,
Written in books, but here surpassed by truth,
The Bachelor Hypolito returns,
And leaves the Gipsy with the Spanish Student

SCENE VI.

A pass in the Guadarrama mountains. Early morning.
A muleteer crosses the stage, sitting sideways on his
mule, and lighting a paper cigar with flint and steel

SONG.

If thou art sleeping, maiden,
   Awake and open thy door,
'T is the break of day, and we must away,
   O'er meadow, and mount, and moor.

Wait not to find thy slippers,
   But come with thy naked feet;
We shall have to pass through the dewy grass,
   And waters wide and fleet.

*(Disappears down the pass.   Enter a Monk.   A Shepherd
appears on the rocks above.)*

MONK.

Ave Maria, gratia plena.   Olá ! good man !

SHEPHERD.

Olá !

MONK.

Is this the road to Segovia ?

SHEPHERD.

It is, your reverence.

MONK.

How far is it ?

SHEPHERD.

I do not know.

MONK.

What is that yonder in the valley ?

SHEPHERD.

San Ildefonso.

MONK.

A long way to breakfast.

SHEPHERD.

Ay, marry.

MONK.

Are there robbers in these mountains ?

SHEPHERD.

Yes, and worse than that.

MONK.

What ?

SHEPHERD.

Wolves.

MONK.

Santa Maria ! Come with me to San Ildefon so, and thou shalt be well rewarded.

SHEPHERD.

What wilt thou give me ?

MONK.

An Agnus Dei and my benediction.

(*They disappear. A mounted Contrabandista passes, wrapped in his cloak, and a gun at his saddle-bow. He goes down the pass singing.*)

SONG.

Worn with speed is my good steed,
And I march me hurried, worried;
Onward, caballito mio,
With the white star in thy forehead!
Onward, for here comes the Ronda,
And I hear their rifles crack!
Ay, jaléo! Ay, ay, jaléo!
Ay, jaléo! They cross our track.

(*Song dies away. Enter* PRECIOSA, *on horseback, attended
by* VICTORIAN, HYPOLITO, DON CARLOS, *and* CHISPA,
on foot, and armed.)

VICTORIAN.

This is the highest point. Here let us rest.
See, Preciosa, see how all about us
Kneeling, like hooded friars, the misty mountains
Receive the benediction of the sun!
O glorious sight!

PRECIOSA.

Most beautiful indeed!

HYPOLITO.

Most wonderful !

VICTORIAN.

And in the vale below,

Where yonder steeples flash like lifted halberds,

San Ildefonso, from its noisy belfries,

Sends up a salutation to the morn,

As if an army smote their brazen shields,

And shouted victory !

PRECIOSA.

And which way lies

Segovia ?

VICTORIAN.

At a great distance yonder.

Dost thou not see it ?

PRECIOSA.

No. I do not see it.

VICTORIAN.

The merest flaw that dents the horizon's edge.

There, yonder !

HYPOLITO.

'T is a notable old town,
Boasting an ancient Roman aqueduct,
And an Alcázar, builded by the Moors,
Wherein, you may remember, poor Gil Blas
Was fed on *Pan del Rey.* O, many a time
Out of its grated windows have I looked
Hundreds of feet plumb down to the Eresma,
That, like a serpent through the valley creeping,
Glides at its foot.

PRECIOSA.

O, yes ! I see it now,
Yet rather with my heart, than with mine eyes,
So faint it is. And, all my thoughts sail thither,
Freighted with prayers and hopes, and forward
urged
Against all stress of accident, as, in
The Eastern Tale, against the wind and tide,
Great ships were drawn to the Magnetic Moun-
tains,

And there were wrecked, and perished in the
.sea! (*She weeps.*)

O gentle spirit! Thou didst bear unmoved
Blasts of adversity and frosts of fate!
But the first ray of sunshine that falls on thee
Melts thee to tears! O, let thy weary heart
Lean upon mine! and it shall faint no more,
Nor thirst, nor hunger; but be comforted
And filled with my affection.

Stay no longer!
My father waits. Methinks I see him there,
Now looking from the window, and now watching
Each sound of wheels or foot-fall in the street,
And saying, "Hark! she comes!" O father!
father!

(*They descend the pass.* CHISPA *remains behind.*)

I have a father, too, but he is a dead one.

Alas and alack-a-day! Poor was I born, and
poor do I remain. I neither win nor lose. Thus
I wag through the world, half the time on foot,
and the other half walking; and always as merry
as a thunder-storm in the night. And so we
plough along, as the fly said to the ox. Who
knows what may happen? Patience, and shuffle
the cards! I am not yet so bald, that you can
see my brains; and perhaps, after all, I shall
some day go to Rome, and come back Saint
Peter. Benedicite!   [*Exit*

(*A pause. Then enter* BARTOLOMÉ *wildly, as if in pur-
suit, with a carbine in his hand.*)

BARTOLOMÉ.

They passed this way! I hear their horses
    hoofs!
Yonder I see them! Come, sweet caramillo,
This serenade shall be the Gipsy's last!
    (*Fires down the pass.*)
Ha! ha! Well whistled, my sweet caramillo!
    30

Well whistled ! — I have missed her ! — O, my
    God !

    (*The shot is returned.*   BARTOLOMÉ *falls.*)

NOTES.

NOTES.

Page 10. *As Lope says.*

"La cólera

de un Español sentado no se templa,

sino le representan en dos horas

hasta el final juicio desde el Génesis."

Lope de Vega.

Page 302. *Abernuncio Satanas.*

"Digo, Señora, respondió Sancho, lo que tengo dicho, que de los azotes abernuncio. Abrenuncio, habeis de decir, Sancho, y no como decis, dijo el Duque." — *Don Quixote*, Part II., ch. 35.

Page 332. *Fray Carrillo.*

The allusion here is to a Spanish Epigram.

"Siempre Fray Carrillo estás

cansándonos acá fuera;

quien en tu celda estuviera

para no verte jamas!"

Böhl de Faber.   Floresta, No. 611.

Page 333.   *Padre Francisco.*

This is from an Italian popular song.

" 'Padre Francesco,

Padre Francesco!'

— Cosa volete del Padre Francesco —

' V' è una bella ragazzina

Che si vuole confessar!'

Fatte l' entrare, fatte l' entrare!

Che la voglio confessare."

*Kopisch.   Volksthümliche Poesien aus allen Mun-
darten Italiens und seiner Inseln,* p. 194.

Page 336.   *Ave! cujus calcem clare.*

From a monkish hymn of the twelfth century, in Sir
Alexander Croke's *Essay on the Origin, Progress, and
Decline of Rhyming Latin Verse,* p. 109.

Page 351.   *The gold of the Busné.*

Busné is the name given by the Gipsies to all who
are not of their race.

Page 354. *Count of the Calés.*

The Gipsies call themselves Calés. See Borrow's valuable and extremely interesting work, *The Zincali; or an Account of the Gipsies in Spain.* London, 1841.

Page 362. *Asks if his money-bags would rise.*

" ¿ Y volviéndome á un lado, ví á un Avariento, que estaba preguntando á otro, (que por haber sido embalsamado, y estar léxos sus tripas no hablaba, porque no habian llegado si habian de resucitar aquel dia todos los enterrados) si resucitarian unos bolsones suyos? " — *El Sueño de las Calaveras.*

Page 362. *And amen! said my Cid Campeador.*

A line from the ancient *Poema del Cid.*

" Amen, dixo Mio Cid el Campeador."

Line 3044.

Page 364. *The river of his thoughts.*

This expression is from Dante ;

" Si che chiaro
Per essa scenda della mente il fiume."

Byron has likewise used the expression; though I do not recollect in which of his poems.

Page 366.   *Mari Franca.*

A common Spanish proverb, used to turn aside a question one does not wish to answer;

> " Porque casó Mari Franca
>   quatro leguas de Salamanca."

Page 368.   *Ay, soft, emerald eyes.*

The Spaniards, with good reason, consider this color of the eye as beautiful, and celebrate it in song; as, for example, in the well known *Villancico;*

> " Ay ojuelos verdes,
>   ay los mis ojuelos,
>   ay hagan los cielos
>   que de mi te acuerdes !
>
>   .   .   .   .
>
>   Tengo confianza
>   de mis verdes ojos."
>   *Böhl de Faber. Floresta,* No. 255.

Dante speaks of Beatrice's eyes as emeralds. *Purga-torio,* xxxi. 116 Lami says, in his *Annotazioni,* " Erano i suoi occhi d' un turchino verdiccio, simile a quel del mare."

Page 371. *The Avenging Child.*
See the ancient Ballads of *El Infante Vengador*, and *Calaynos.*

Page 372. *All are sleeping.*
From the Spanish. *Böhl's Floresta*, No. 282.

Page 402. *Good night.*
From the Spanish ; as are likewise the songs immediately following, and that which commences the first scene of Act III.

Page 435. *The evil eye.*
" In the Gitano language, casting the evil eye is called *Querelar nasula*, which simply means making sick, and which, according to the common superstition, is accomplished by casting an evil look at people, especially children, who, from the tenderness of their constitution, are supposed to be more easily blighted than those of a more

mature age. After receiving the evil glance, they fall
sick, and die in a few hours.

" The Spaniards have very little to say respecting the
evil eye, though the belief in it is very prevalent, espe-
cially in Andalusia, amongst the lower orders. A stag's
horn is considered a good safeguard, and on that account
a small horn, tipped with silver, is frequently attached to
the children's necks by means of a cord braided from the
hair of a black mare's tail. Should the evil glance be
cast, it is imagined that the horn receives it, and instantly
snaps asunder. Such horns may be purchased in some
of the silversmiths' shops at Seville."

Borrow's Zincali. Vol. I. ch. ix.

Page 436. *On the top of a mountain I stand.*

This and the following scraps of song are from Bor
row's *Zincali; or an Account of the Gipsies in Spain.*

The Gipsy words in the same scene may be thus inter-
preted :

John-Dorados, pieces of gold.

Pigeon, a simpleton.

In your morocco, stripped.

Doves, sheets.

Moon, a shirt.

Chirelin, a thief.

Murcigalleros, those who steal at night-fall.

Rastilleros, foot-pads.

Hermit, highway-robber.

Planets, candles.

Commandments, the fingers.

Saint Martin asleep, to rob a person asleep.

Lanterns, eyes.

Goblin, police officer.

Papagayo, a spy.

Vineyards and Dancing John, to take flight.

Page 458. *If thou art sleeping, maiden.*

From the Spanish; as is likewise the song of the Contrabandista on page 169.

END OF VOL. I.

Printed in Great Britain
by Amazon

37157770R00274